Kabbala

Kabbala

A Dictionary of
Terms, Practices and Applications

Rephael Yedidya

Astrolog Publishing House Ltd

Cover Design: Na'ama Yaffe

© Astrolog Publishing House Ltd. 2004

P. O. Box 1123, Hod Hasharon 45111, Israel
Tel: 972-9-7412044
Fax: 972-9-7442714

ISBN 965-494-190-2

Published by
Astrolog Publishing House 2004

Contents

The Tree of Life 9

The Ten Sefirot 9

Keter 11

Chochma 13

Binah 14

Chesed 15

Gevurah 17

Tif'Eret 18

Netzah 20

Hod 21

Yesod 22

Malchut 23

Kabalistic numerology 27

Kabalistic Astrology 41

Moon 42

Sun 43

Mercury 44

Venus 45

Mars 46

Jupiter 47

Saturn 48

Zodiac signs 49

Aries 53

Leo 53

Sagittarius 54

Taurus 55

Virgo 55

Capricorn 56

Gemini 57

Libra 57

Aquarius 58

Cancer 59

Scorpio 59

Pisces 60

A Dictionary of Terms, Practices and Applications 63

Animals

Ants

Asthma

Back

Bad breath

Barren Woman

Bees

Birth

Blood

Boils

Breast Feeding

Breasts

Burial of a pregnant woman

Burns

Children

Cough

Crying

Deafness

Diarrhea

Disease

Dogs

Dream Signs

Dreams

Drinking

Earaches

Eating

Elements

Enemy

Epilepsy

Eyes

Fasting

Feet
Fire
Fish
Fleas
Food and Drink
Gems
Gold
Head
Heart
Hernia
Holy Names
House
Impotence
Jaundice
Jealousy
Kidney stones
Knowledge
Ligaments
Liver
Loneliness
Loss
Love
Lungs
Lupine
Madness
Malaria
Man and Wife
Mandrakes
Marriage
Mating
Memory
Names
Negotiations
Oaths
Oils

Old Age
Plague
Pox
Pregnancy
Prison
Proverbs
Rags
Rheumatism
Salt
Sea
Seed
Skin
Sleep
Snakes
Snoring
Speech
Spleen
Stomach
Strawberries
Success
Sweat
Teeth
Throat
Trees
Urine
Venom
Weather
Will
Wisdom
Witchcraft
Worms
Worry
Wounds

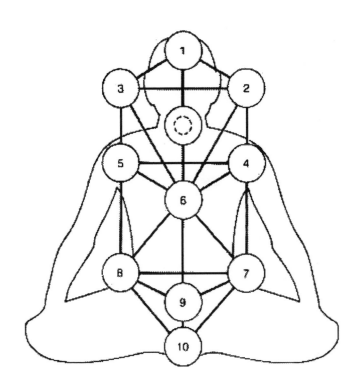

The Tree of Life

The Ten Sefirot

The Ten Sefirot are a prime concept in the Kabalistic worldview. Before the material world in which we live was created, the Lord created many higher ethereal worlds; these became the "plan" after which our own world was patterned, a reflection as well as result of it. Every Sefira is a level of substantiality and of divine will solidified. The Sefirot act as intermediary realms between an infinite, eternal God and a finite creation, just as veils or filters before a great light create a pattern of shadows on a wall.

The visual representation of the Ten Sefirot is called the Tree of Life, a construct with a distinct top and bottom, left, center and right. The Right represents expansion and compassion, encompassing the Sefirot of Chochma, Chesed and Netzah; the Left, contraction and judgment, including the Sefirot of Binah, Gevurah and Hod; the Center, to harmony between the two, in the Sefirot of Keter, Tif'Eret, Yesod and Malchut. The Tree of Life is also superimposed in the human body, with each Sefira taking its place in an organ or limb.

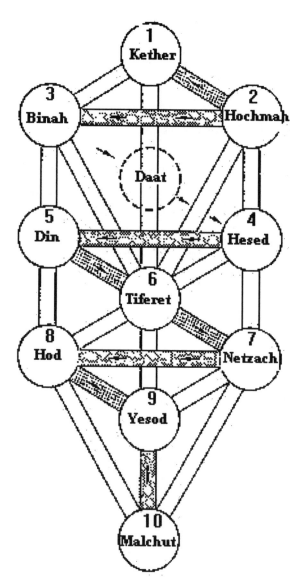

The Ten Sefirot

The higher levels of existence also have an influence on the souls and bodies of men and women here on this earth. Since all divine light comes down to and into us through the Sefirot, the light that shines in certain individuals' spirits differs in its Sefira of origin from that of others. By knowing the numerical value of a person's name, we may often locate the Sefira that governs him in body and soul, and learn much about his ways and desires. God created the world through speech and naming, turning pattern into being - so does the naming of a man or woman make manifest in them the pattern of the Sefirot and allow a glimpse inside.

Keter

"Keter" means "crown" – the Sefira of the all-encompassing, unfathomable, primordial Divine Will, the Reason of Reasons, the cause of creation, in which the goodness of all things is revealed. Keter is the Sefira of spirit – pure spirit. Its area is the head - the inside, outside and its surrounding space; its color is white; its symbol is the swastika.

In humans, the Sefira of Keter represents the aspiration and desire for excellence and perfection, originality and creativity, spirituality and disregard of the material, a loving will to give without limits, boundless compassion and forgiveness, and knowledge. A soul of the Keter Sefira suffers greatly if its body acts against these traits.

There are no physical conditions relating to the Sefira of Keter. It is a wholly spiritual sphere, accounting for perfect health.

The origin of the Sefira of Keter was in the creation of the divine light, which before Genesis filled the whole of the universe with God's eternal goodness. The first Sefira was created when God wished to have something with which to share His abundant goodness, a thing that must be willing to receive the light, since in the spiritual worlds, nothing is possible by force. Thus, God blocked off some of His light, creating a place within the cosmos containing no light. This space became the first vessel in the world, the first thing which had a beginning, and consequently, an end.

The Keter is the first thing created from nothing - after that, there was no creation from void. It exists both in the spiritual and material worlds.

Some say that, at some point, the Keter became eager to share the light that was flowing into it without limit, but had none to share it with, being the only vessel in the universe. Since it could not participate in creation and pass its light on, the Keter sank into the distress of one who receives much but gives nothing. In response, it retracted, refusing the light given it. This is known as the "Breaking of Vessels".

With the light gone, however, the Keter was now overwhelmed with need, just as a man dying of thirst wishes for water. The need to receive was a hundred times greater than before the blocking of the light. Since such great need could not exist so close to the infinite, the Keter was removed from its place and distanced from God, and this removal led to the creation of new vessels to receive the divine light.

This process is repeated with any vessel that feels the power of the light that fills it, and too quickly wishes to share it with others, so fiercely that it refuses to receive until it can give.

Keter is the archetype of humanity, our beginnings and roots, the simplest and most primal of states. For this reason, it is sometimes called "Ayin," or nothingness.

Chochma

Chochma is wisdom, the sphere 'beneath' Keter on the Tree of Life. It is the beginning of all wisdom that ever was and ever will be, and is associated with spiritual will. Its color is the first to emerge from blackness - some believe gray, some, blue. Its symbol is the inner robe; its place in the body is the right lobe of the brain, responsible for intelligence, analysis and conception.

The Sefira of Chochma stands for scientific discovery and invention, for liveliness, nobility, refinement and purity, for thought, and the wish to give. But wisdom is not always a guarantee of intelligence. For this reason the Sefira of Chochma is related to diseases like insanity, delusion and depression as well as false prophecy. Its positive aspects, however, relate to physical and spiritual renewal.

Chochma was created out of Keter as the first creation of one thing from another rather than from Void. Thus it is so very high and refined that no physical being can reach it. This Sefira is still not Creation, though, but only the wish to create, to discover and receive the divine light. As the beginning of creation, it is called "Yesh".

Thus Chochma is one of the roots of creation, the Father of the Sefirot which is constantly renewing all that is through its intercourse with the second pillar, the Sefira of Binah. One of its facets turns to receive the divine light from Keter; but the other turns down and shines light on all the other Sefirot.

Binah

Binah means understanding. This Mother Sefira is located 'under' Chochma on the Tree of Light, in the body residing in the left lobe of the brain responsible for intuition, emotion and artistic expression. Binah is the Mother Sefira, since it is here that creation finally comes into being, with creation and the discovery of the divine light above all else. This vessel feels worthy of existence only if it receives the light.

This element of self-sacrifice in the Sefira of Binah is what lets the divine light shine through into the act of creation, realizing the potential treasure within Chochma. As Keter is the Sefira of Will and Chochma is the Sefira of Idea, so this is the Sefira of execution. Its color is green like growing grass, its symbol, the outer robe.

In humans, Binah embodies creativity, fertility, expression – the will to make, to influence, determination and no compromise, self-sacrifice and altruism. But understanding is also the beginning of all soothing and healing, and those rich in Binah know to turn to God to find comfort in harsh judgment. Physically, it influences either the renewal and swift healing of wounds, or in its negative side, self-destruction, the force opposite to creation.

Chesed

Chesed means "grace", "love" or "mercy", and this Sefira stands for love – individual love between humans, or the pure love of God which brings each creature closer to the divine light. It is positioned 'below' Binah on the Tree of Life, and begins a new cycle of Sefirot of providence, beyond pure spirit.

The effects of Chesed are felt in all things that are white. Its many actions in the cosmos relate to granting us Godly grace and love, and drawing us closer to Binah, since love leads to understanding. It also governs the Sefira of Gevurah that is under it, tempering justice with love. Chesed teaches us to love God boundlessly and without question.

The color belonging to Chesed is white, its symbol is the scepter, its area in the body is the right shoulder and the right arm, which acts and gives out, and the time it is associated with is Sunday.

In humans, Chesed is the Sefira of mercy and giving, of justice and honesty, humility, good deeds and loyalty. It commands love between people and places, good homes, peace and fertility. Those blessed by the Sefira of Chesed enjoy success in peacemaking and negotiation and find spiritual as well as material wealth wherever they turn, overcoming danger and using their energies for the best causes. Physically, Chesed is related to childbearing and the health of children, to swift healing and peace of mind.

It is said that the Sefira of Chesed relates to the male aspect of the Tree of Life, and was embodied in the soul of Abraham, who was gracious even in the face of evil, and abundant in love. As Abraham was the one who discovered the spiritual power of Chesed, which is the seed to all the Sefirot that follow, so was he the seed of Israel.

Gevurah

Gevurah means "power", yet this Sefira's true meaning is actually closer to judgment. Mainly a Sefira of negative energy, Gevurah is the burning side of the divine light, God's wrath turned against man, inciting strife and destruction, even thinning the flow of the light, all to pass unyielding judgment untempered by mercy. Related to strife and disagreement, Gevurah emphasizes the differences God created between his children.

Gevurah represents bravery, stubbornness and pride, anger, sometimes cruelty and bloodlust, hate and envy. Many more negative qualities are embodied in it as well – corruption, false oath and treachery, and a stormy temper touched by lust. This is the Sefira that awakens in men the desire for material possessions and for excess. Yet it also stands for fierce justice. Physically it might entail addiction, but a person under its influence who learns to restrain the rage in him can become harmless, and a fast healer.

As might be expected, the color of Gevurah is red, and it is tied strongly to the mystery of fire's power and allure, its symbol is the spear, its day is Monday, and in the body, it relates to the left arm and to the left side, which is considered impure.

In the Sefira of Gevurah lies the source of the soul of Isaac, who suffered from the strictness of judgment all his life, as long as he labored to limit Gevurah's polluting power on him. He was almost sacrificed by his father, was deceived by his sons, and in his old age was stricken blind. Despite this all, he consistently fought with judgment's power, to balance its spiritual energy with the mellowing influence of mercy. His struggle indeed bore fruit – in Tif'Eret, the Sefira following Gevurah, and in his son Jacob whose soul was made within it.

Tif'Eret

The Sefira Tif'Eret, or "glory", is the final stage before the creation of our flawed material world, and as such, is 'lowly' compared to Gevurah, which is 'above' it on the Tree of Life. Tif'Eret is sometimes seen as a framework in which six other Sefirot – Chesed, Gevurah, Tif'Eret, Netzah, Hod and Yesod – reside. It is the role of those six engines of creation to ease and dilute the divine light, lest it raze the physical world with its sheer glory and power. It reveals to us the glory of all creatures as created by God.

As Chesed's grace tempers justice, so Tif'Eret mingles justice and love. It is told that at first, God created a world that was all love and all mercy, but that world could not last because nothing can be loving and just without justice. Then He created a world that was all justice, which could not last because justice without mercy is mere cruelty. Thus did God finally create our new world, placing it under the Sefira of Tif'Eret – justice and love intertwined.

Tif'Eret also has a role in beauty and in the study of Torah; as it combines justice and love, so it combines red and white, fire and water. Through its union with the Sefira of Malchut, souls come into being.

The body part of Tif'Eret is the torso, and thus, as the center of the body and the Tree of Life alike, all other Sefirot are linked to it. Its color is the yellow of gemstones, its time, Tuesday, its symbol, the rosy cross.

In humans, Tif'Eret is the Sefira of beauty, discovery and knowledge of secrets both lofty and earthly, and of honor and generosity. Those who feel its influence enjoy good friends, financial success and often hints of divine blessing. They can overcome all enemies, yet, they may gain such enemies easily. Physically, it is said that vegetarianism suits both the bodies and spirits of those under its mantle.

The embodiment of Tif'Eret is in Jacob, bearing both Abraham's grace and the justice dealt to Yitzhak, and creating the bridge between them as a whole and unified person.

Netzah

Netzah means "eternity", or more often, "triumph". It is a reminder that what will be will be, and God's will, in the end, shall be triumphant. 'Below' the Sefirot of divine judgment, mercy and their balance, it is the first of three Sefirot of the "actual" and the "is", coming closer to the material world.

Netzah resides in the right leg, which is firm, its symbol is the girdle, its day is Wednesday and it is associated with no color.

Souls under the influence of Netzah are characterized by determination and drive, the power of seeds sown, achieving goals and love of life and pleasure. They find peace from a position of strength, success with chosen partners, fertility, beauty and grace. Physically it relates to sexual prowess and the birth of many children, and to healthy *joi de vivre*.

Netzah passes the positive energies of the right side from the pure divine heights to the material world. It did so through the prophet whose soul came from Netzah – Moses, who brought the Torah down from Mt. Sinai, from God to his people.

Hod

Hod, which means "splendor", is the beginning of the final channel of the divine light into the material. In splendor, God-given beauty is manifested in the physical world. While it is true that Hod resides in the left side, which attracts negative energies, this only proves that even that which might seem negative and evil is ultimately a part of God's own divine plan to further the beauty of his creation.

The Sefira of Hod belongs to the left leg, its symbol is spells, its color, orange, its day, Thursday. Hod is Thought, which emerges from Memory, the Sefira of Yesod.

Individuals touched by Hod are blessed in speech and prayer, able to teach, govern and make peace between their fellow men. They make good advisors, writers and artists inclined towards the beauty of expression. They spread love and undo bad intention. Physically, they may suffer often from a blocked nose, and are prone to fits of anger quickly replaced by calm.

Hod was revealed in the soul of Aaron, the brother of Moses, who was a teacher and peacemaker to the people of Israel, ever working to mend the flaws the negative left energies of Hod caused in them. Preaching of love freely given, true constant prayer from deep within the heart, and peace between all men on earth, he was a man of great splendor indeed.

Yesod

The last of the Sefirot of the divine, Yesod means "foundation". Yesod is the final channel of the divine light into our world, and serving as a channel is its entire function, which is nonetheless important. Yesod acts as a regulator and gate. It is as the male seed flowing into the female material world, and there also, in the contact between it and the final, worldly Sefira of Malchut, are born human souls.

Individuals under the influence of Yesod are as the channel through which blessings and plenty flow to others, the symbol of righteousness and good omens. They love the company of others, tend to travel often, yield before higher powers and have the strength to rule. However they often find themselves dependant on divine grace, or involved in strife. Physically, Yesod relates to the mouth - purity of thought will lead to perfect health, while scheming and foul words, to sickness.

It is contact with the Sefira of Yesod that reminds us of God's constant connection to all his creation, which can never be separated from him. It is, therefore, the purpose of all spiritual and mystical quests.

Yesod resides in the body in the genitalia, from which come the material part of new life, its day is Friday, its color purple, and its symbol, sandals, relating to travel.

The soul of Joseph the dreamer came from this Sefira, for he was the channel through which God gave omens for the future, and through which wealth came to the people of Egypt in the years of famine.

Malchut

The final Sefira, Malchut is "kingdom", which is no longer a higher level of existence or place. Malchut is the Sefira of the physical world where God's creatures reside. At last the divine light is brought to the material plane – revealed in the inner fire that gives life to all. We cannot see the divine light, but we can sense its existence in life itself. In the Sefira of Malchut, in life, the majesty of God is fully revealed.

In all the Sefirot above Malchut, the light is not only received but given as well – it is in their nature that they act as channels for the light to reach Malchut. Therefore they remain more spirit than matter. The closer they come to Malchut, however, the thicker and more material they become. Malchut is the thickest of all.

In our material world, the need to receive the light is at its peak, for all the light that flows through the Sefirot above comes to it. The light flows down to us by God's grace. To avoid what happened to Keter at its beginning – the denial of light we feel unworthy of – men labor in this

Sefira to do good deeds and purify their souls. Thus, what is given by grace becomes granted by right - the just man's right to the divine light. Only there can the soul be made clearer, because of our need to work hard to achieve the light and give as well as receive. Only in Malchut can the soul begin its journey back up to the higher worlds.

Malchut is also the spiritual within the physical – God's presence in the heart of every human being. *Shechina* is called the feminine element of Malchut, God's feminine face, peace and religious purity, the uplifting to spiritual heights.

The soul that embodied Malchut is that of King David, and the Star of David is its symbol. It is associated with Saturday, God's day of rest, the material world having been created. Its symbol is the complete circle; it is associated with a myriad of colors, black, green, red and blue. In the body, it resides in the feet, which connect man to the ground. Malchut embodies all traits – it has no dominant influence of its own on men's natures.

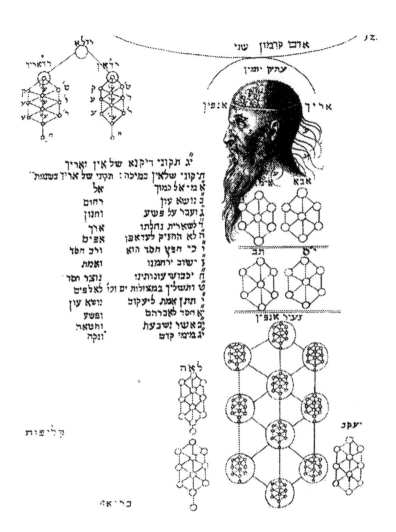

אדם קדמון שני ‎12.

עתיק יומין

אריך א:פין

יג תקוני דיקנא של אין יאריך

תקוני שלאין במיכה : תקוני של אריך בשמות

אל ‎א מי אל כמוך
רחום ‎ב נשא עון
וחנון ‎ג ועבר על פשע
ארך ‎ד לשארית נחלתו
אפים ‎ה לא החזיק לעד אפו
ורב חסד ‎ו כי חפץ חסד הוא
ואמת ‎ז ישוב ירחמנו
נצר חסד ‎ח יכבוש עונותינו
‎ט ותשליך במצולות ים וכל לאלפים
נשא עון ‎י תתן אמת ליעקב
ופשע ‎יא חסד לאברהם
וחטאה ‎יב אשר נשבעת
ונקה ‎יג מימי קדם

אבא

אמא

לב

זעיר אנפין

לאה

קליפות

יעקב

בריאה

Kabalistic numerology

In Kabalistic philosophy, numbers and letters are things of power.

Each individual upon birth is given a name made up of letters which each have their own energies and powers. This refers to the first name alone, since family names are later additions, artificial and common, often stemming from a person's profession or hometown. However, when forming a first name, the power of letters affects the character of the name-bearer, much as strokes of color form a painting or strung notes a melody. In our names, the connection we have to the Ten Sefirot is also concealed.

As each letter designates a numerical value, one can add up those values to find his or her number, which, as a manifestation of the name, has a profound influence on personality, physical traits and place in the world.

The power of numbers originates in the power of letters and is similar to it. Numbers are also part of the language in which God spoke to the world, which He passed on to us so that, through it, we may learn the secrets of His creation.

By the number that a person's name forms, we may learn from which of the Sefirot his soul came into the world, and so picture his character and traits.

To find your number in Kabalistic numerology, use the following grouping of letters:

A, J, S – value of 1

B, K, T – value of 2

C, L, U – value of 3

D, M, V – value of 4

E, N, W – value of 5

F, O, X – value of 6

G, P, Y – value of 7

H, Q, Z – value of 8

I, R – value of 9

Add up the values of the letters of your name until you reach a single-number result, the meaning of which is to be found below. The exception is thirteen, which is a unique number whose digits needn't be added up. What if you come up with a two-digit number – do you knock off the second digit? No. Add up the numbers to reach a single-number result

$$8+6+5+4= 23 = 2+3 = 5$$

$$1+9+2+6+4+3 = 25 = 2+5 = 7$$

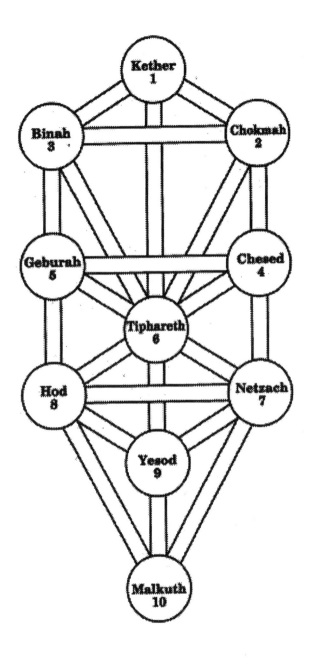

1

One is wholeness and uniqueness, leadership, success, courage and confidence, optimism and originality, secrets revealed, a career, a circle completed.

Connected to the Sefira of Keter, to Leo on the Zodiac and to the moon, it is represented by a single point linked to no other – one is a lone whole, complete in itself.

On the negative side, a person whose numerological result is one may, if he does not use his energies well, become selfish, manipulative, lacking patience and confidence. Where the balance may tilt is completely up to the individual and his or her deeds.

2

Two is connected to the Sefira of Chochma, and thus to sensitivity and gentleness, fragile beauty, feminine strength and diplomatic ability. Hesitation and lack of confidence also come with this number.

Two is related to Cancer on the Zodiac, and to the planet Venus through its feminine influence.

Two is represented by the line drawn between two points, hence its ties to mediating. Wisdom is seeing the two sides of a coin, and sharing can only be achieved when there is a second being to share with.

The negative influence of this number may be felt in constant worry, lack of emotional, mental and physical balance, unjustified fears, or plain apathy.

3

Three symbolizes practical thinking, the elements of air, water and fire, intelligence, talent in the fields of sound and shape – music and visual arts – to restrain passion, optimism, giving, independence and wealth.

Three is connected to the planet Jupiter, and Sagittarius on the Zodiac, as well as the Sefira of Binah which is the root of creativity. Its symbol is the triangle.

Negative uses of this number's energies lead to egoism, lack of passion, sadness, nervousness and a tendency to gamble.

4

Four stands for spiritual roots, strong ties to home and community, love of work, determination and originality, strong will, perfectionism and overcoming obstacles.

This number relates to the Sefira of Chesed, the planet Uranus and to Aquarius on the Zodiac. Four is represented by the square, the greatest symbol of stability and strength, as well as order and organization.

As its positive side is success, the negative is failure, as well as violence, stubbornness, rebellion and lack of trust.

5

Five is connected to the Sefira of Gevurah, the symbol of creation, judgment, faith in the senses, travel and trade, independence, sensuality, courage, breaking the routine.

Five is influenced by the planet Mercury and by Gemini on the Zodiac, it is represented by the pentacle, which also represents the five limbs that lead man's life – two feet for travel, two hands for creation, and a head for sensing and knowing.

On the negative side, which those touched by Gevurah

must be aware of, this number symbolizes irresponsibility, deceit, rumors and slander, bitterness and misery, lack of conscience and shallowness.

6

Six symbolizes grace and beauty, health, home and family, love and friendship, principles, peacefulness, advancement, sharing and giving, and respect for one's fellow beings.

Six is influenced by Libra on the Zodiac, the Sefira of Tif'Eret and the planet Venus. It is represented by the Star of David, a double triangle – at its peak in spirit, at its base in man, as appropriate for the number of the Sefira that is at the heart of the Tree of Life.

This number has few negative effects – narrow-mindedness, envy and strife.

7

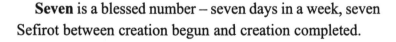

Seven is a blessed number – seven days in a week, seven Sefirot between creation begun and creation completed.

It is linked to the Sefira of Netzah, symbolizing abstract thinking, mysticism, understanding and all that is spiritual, marriage and partnership, as well as loneliness, sacrifice, inner peace and high sensitivity. Seven bears contradictions within it – a number of mystery.

This number relates to Pisces on the Zodiac, and to the planet Neptune. Representing it is the Seal of Solomon, the Star of David with a point at its heart to symbolize the spirit.

On its negative side, it is tied to escapism and wantonness.

8

Eight is the combination of spirituality and materialism, life and death – the continuity of the human species, also thinking big, authority and responsibility, determination, positive approach and aspiration.

It relates to the Sefira of Hod, to Saturn, and to Capricorn on the Zodiac. It is represented by a cube.

The negative energies of this number might result in lack of motivation, material greed, dependence and irresponsibility, shallowness and overly harsh judgment.

9

Nine, the number of the months before birth, symbolizes all that is good in the world – fairness, mercy, kindness of heart, soft character, willingness to help, true principles and tolerance, a vivid imagination, and travel, as well as abstract thinking.

This number, however, is not without faults – egoism, manipulation, hurting others through hate and jealousy, greed.

It is represented by the triple trinity – three times three make nine.

Nine is tied to the Sefira of Yesod, the final channel of the light, to the planet Mars and to Aries on the Zodiac.

10

Ten is a non-number – $1+0 = 1$, and so we return to number **one** and complete the cycle, from Keter to Malchut, from God to creation.

13

Thirteen in Jewish mysticism is a unique number, as it is in Christianity. Yet while Christianity branded it evil, in Kabalistic numerology, the number 13 is a symbol of love and unity. One whose name adds up to 13 is ruled by these traits, giving wealth to all without asking for any in return.

A person's numerological result is also the indication of his or her Sefira. The two influences cannot be viewed apart, but only as a whole, along with astrological influences.

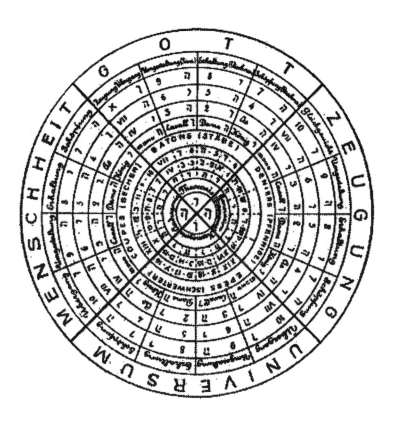

Kabalistic Astrology

As opposed to ordinary astrology, in Jewish mysticism, it is not the stars and heavenly bodies that determine the fate of men. Quite differently, it is the higher Sefirot and spiritual worlds that influence both human beings and the movements in the heavens. We may see human destiny echoed in the stars, but will not see it dictated there.

The Jewish calendar is based upon both the sun and moon, unlike the calendar of any other monotheistic religion, thus the Kabalistic view of astrology is both more whole and comprehensive.

Kabalistic astrology, it is said, began with Abraham, who received from God Himself his secret knowledge of communing with the Sefirot and seeing in the stars. Most of those secrets he passed to Isaac his son, who passed them to Jacob, from whom they passed to all his sons and to the twelve Hebrew tribes.

According to Kabbala, the influence of the seven lower Sefirot is felt through that of seven heavenly bodies – the moon, the sun, Venus, Mars, Mercury, Saturn and Jupiter, and these in turn influence the twelve signs of the Zodiac. Each planet influences two signs, and the sun and moon influence one each. The signs are tied, also, to the four elements – earth, air, fire and water, as they are in ordinary astrology.

Moon

The influence on the moon is that of the Sefirot of Malchut and Binah, and also Netzah. Those born under it are cunning and clever, though sometimes indecisive, tending to changes and revolutions, quick growth but just as quick wilting. On the negative side, they may become dreamy and detached from worldly business. The moon has a powerful effect on women.

The moon is a symbol of the cycles of nature, death and renewal, ebb and tide. Thus it is tied to duality, rot and ugliness, waning and lacking but also beauty, goodness, grace, art and fertility. It is also a planet of defense, and of pagan witchcraft.

The moon influences the eyes, the lungs and throat, the womb and the left side of the body. It causes restlessness, changing moods, tiredness at times, and extremity in sensation.

Sun

The nature of the sun is influenced by the Sefira of Tif'Eret, and to a lesser extent, Hod. It is responsible for light and for spirit, the grace of God and men. Its place is in the center of the other planets, marking it as a sign of both judgment and grace, life and death, as the sun both lights the world and may burn it, depending on the use of its energies.

Those born under it are clear of mind and heart and speak truth, wise, learned and gracious, doing good deeds and always speaking their mind, with a love of knowledge. They are often leaders of men destined for greatness – kings are of the sun, and kingly honor and splendor, overcoming foes and giving to the needy, love of nature and its wisdom. On the negative side, they may make financial mistakes, surrender easily or become overly proud.

The sun influences the heart, the right eye, the brain, arteries and the right half of the body, and all diseases originating in the mouth. Crystals and gems have a soothing influence on those under the sign of the sun, who are almost always healthy, rarely fall ill, and when they do, heal quickly and completely.

Mercury

Mercury is influenced mainly by the Sefira of Chesed but also by Tif'Eret and Yesod. It is a positive planet, kind to the spirit, but representing above all the world of logical thought. Born under Mercury are individuals with high abilities of verbal and written expression. They are cunning and plotting but are also fountains of good advice, being balanced and thoughtful. They make good artists and are skilled in languages as well as negotiation, are full of initiative and determination, and love travel. It is said they fare well as traders, making their own living. On its negative side, Mercury stands for a quick temper leading easily to fighting.

The influence of Mercury is over the tongue and mouth and the ligaments, and sometimes the bloodstream, as well as muscular control. It also relates to mental conditions such as depression. Individuals under its influence appear physically and mentally frail, which they usually over-come.

Venus

The nature of Venus is influenced by the Sefira of Chesed – a positive planet regulating lust and desire into the purity of love and attraction and the will to bring new life. Those under its influence are cheery and without a worry on their minds, loving life, laughter and music, living lightly and joyfully. They never experience financial troubles since they know no greed, love their fellow men, are masters of diplomacy, and balance spiritualism and materialism.

Venus is the planet of love and beauty, of attraction, fertility, creation, destiny and balance, uprising of the spirit. Venus influences the liver, the man's seed, and all bodily fluids. It relates to diseases in the kidneys and genitalia, but also to fertility and sensuality, and to physical renewal. Those influenced by Venus have a gift for herbal healing.

Mars

Mars is influenced mainly by the Sefira of Netzah, but also by Gevurah and Chesed. It is the planet of hell's fire, a burning sign of corruption and harm symbolizing destruction and famine, strife, bloodshed and war, competition, parting and death.

Those under its influence are stubborn and powerful, quick-tempered individuals with little love for peace or wisdom, or for religious worship. They are sharp-tongued and may be violent, losing control of their anger and powerful will. They wish to fight and rule by force, tend to jealousy and anger that breeds hate, and may fall into addiction and lust, or even crime.

The influence of Chesed, however, may mend the bad qualities of this planet, turning the will of those under it to positive avenues, such as friendly contests, law-keeping, and even medicine – positive dealing with blood.

Under Mars' influence are the ligaments, the right nostril, the kidneys and genitalia, and it relates to fever, pox, burns, paranoia and madness. The anger it incites in hearts causes mental and physical imbalance, leading sometimes to terror of disease, and sometimes to addiction to alcohol. Those born under it respond well to medical treatment, however.

Jupiter

The nature of Jupiter relates to the Sefirot of Hod, Tif'Eret and Yesod. Those born under it are God-fearing, wise, just and of keen judgment, giving and assuring peace and security. They are kind of heart and soul, humble and faithful yet authoritative, speakers of truth, and full of joy. They are rich in knowledge as well and raise successful children, themselves often finding great success in positions of authority.

Greatest of the planets, Jupiter stands for peace, justice, freedom of body and mind, long life and fertility, as well as material riches, for a search for the wondrous and beautiful, optimism, adventure, love and honor.

Jupiter influences the liver, the left ear and the ribs, as well as a child's physical development, and diseases of the blood. But it also grants a feeling of health, strength and good spirits of the body, and to complete healing, influenced positively by a sapphire gemstone.

Saturn

Saturn is related to the Sefira of Yesod above all, but to Netzah and Hod as well, and is concerned with integration. It is mostly a negative planet in Kabbala, influencing those who are slow learners, often lazy and tend to hold grudges, but who live in great material wealth, are pessimistic, suspicious and desire to rule others. Saturn symbolizes grief and mourning, destruction and death, appointed over worry and ill advice, thirst and hunger. It is the origin of petty strife between petty men.

However Saturn also has a positive aspect, which teaches determination and discipline, and grants strength to bear hardship. Some view the suffering it causes as a test of mettle, or necessary to cleanse the soul that must endure it.

Saturn influences the bones, gall-bladder, the bladder and the right ear, relating to chronic illnesses, bleeding, pains in the legs, madness and leprosy, and to high sensitivity to disease. Good deeds, it is said, remove all these dangers.

There are three additional planets in the solar system – Uranus, Neptune and Pluto, all of which are under the influence of the higher Sefirot, Keter, Chochma and Binah. However, because of their distance from Earth, Kabbala decrees them to have little to no effect.

Zodiac signs

In addition to the stars, or rather under their influence, are the Zodiac signs. They also have an influence on the people on this earth, but Kabbala decrees that that influence is not total. Fate is mutable; good deeds may provide a remedy for ill fortune, and a person born under one sign may acquire the tendencies and traits of another.

The mystic lore of the Kabbala tells us that the signs were created when the lower six Sefirot, Chesed, Gevurah, Tif'Eret, Netzah, Hod and Yesod, shone light down on the six planets, Saturn, Jupiter, Mars, Venus, Mercury and the sun. Out of this were made six signs. The light was then reflected back to the Sefirot and on its way up created six more signs.

The signs of the Zodiac are divided between the natures of the four elements – fire, air, water and earth. They influence the people born under those signs, and especially their relations with each other.

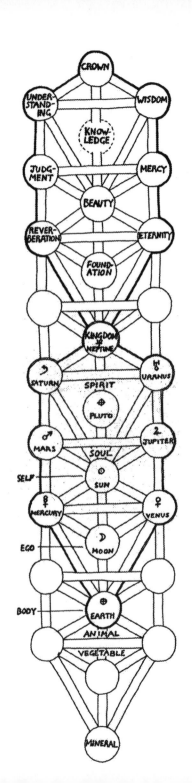

The fire signs are Aries, Leo and Sagittarius. Those under these signs are very compatible with wind signs, raising happy families, overcoming obstacles and loving each other to their dying day. Water signs, however, would prove too dominant in the relationship, much as water puts out fire, and with earth signs they would endure a hard life. Two fire signs would hardly be able to keep up a relationship or marriage, since they would constantly seek to outdo each other.

Aries

Born under the Aries sign are fine, courageous individuals, disciplined and ready to tackle any danger and survive all, but quick to rage and at times vain. Good looking, honest and intelligent, they speak well before an audience, enjoy telling others what to do, and are skilled at negotiating. They tend more towards anger and jealousy than towards joy or mercy, however, they may be self-centered, and are loved by few and envied by many, even though they maintain a sharp sense of humor. Women are more trusting and talkative. Their planet is Mars and they are under the influence of the Sefira of Chesed. Aries stands for the head.

Leo

Under Leo are people of power, who usually gain fame and riches. They are self-controlled and self-confident natural leaders, brave problem-solvers, and noble of heart and mind, whose voice is often heard and whose words are honest. They enjoy work and are dedicated to it and driven, and sometimes take great risks to achieve their goals, but few can harm them and almost all honor them. Women tend to be loners at times, pure and gracious, beautiful and proud-looking. They are associated with the sun and tied to the Sefira of Hod. Leo is the sign of the heart and back.

Sagittarius

The sign Sagittarius promises a great upheaval somewhere in the lives of those born under it, either disastrous or greatly beneficial, and usually unexpected. They are destined to wander far, being adventurous and interested in others, and eventually reach success. These are loyal, talkative and merry types, lovers of life, givers and sharers who support their fellow humans. They are peace-lovers and peacemakers, full of knowledge, moral, outspoken and enjoy making a good impression. Though they are very patient, once that patience runs out they can be cruel. Women enjoy action and movement, have emotional, expressive gazes, and run the risk of depression, mental instability or adultery. Their planet is Jupiter and their Sefira is Tif'Eret. Sagittarius is the sign of the pelvis and liver.

The earth signs are Taurus, Virgo and Capricorn. A pairing of two earth signs is ill-advised – as the earth stands still so would their lives, and as the earth takes in the dead, so would death's shadow loom over them.

Taurus

Under Taurus are successful, joyful people, possessed of pleasant voices and physical beauty, lovers of song and music and the company of the opposite sex. They like being praised, and usually lead good, profitable lives. Men are patient and overcome hardships easily, are practical and firmly grounded in reality, and have the intelligence to achieve their goals, but may be hampered by pride. Sometimes they may be foolish and tend to commit adultery. Women enjoy material wealth but are only truly happy when touching upon the spiritual as well, and tend to be superstitious. Their planet is Venus, their sign represents the neck and throat, and their Sefira is Gevurah.

Virgo

Virgo is the sign of cunning people who gain success and honor through their wits. They have common sense and know the way to wealth even through the lower paths, and tend to spend their wealth happily and with little doubts or regrets. Men and women both are kind, but tend to linger on details and are very serious. Men are thorough and competent, studious and stubborn, responsible, demand perfection of others and are skeptical and extremely careful. Women are modest and quiet and enjoy traveling and walking, and call few other women friends. Their sign represents the internal organs, their Sefira is Yesod and they are tied to the moon.

Capricorn

Capricorn is a sign of the studious and clever, who, if also lucky, find wealth wherever they turn, and are thus often rich. They very close with their families, even if they may at times return ill favor and are willing to do whatever is necessary to gain what they wish, mostly through hard work and great practicality. Routine and appearances are important to them. The men of this sign can be lustful. Their planet is Saturn, their sign is tied to the knees, skin and bones and their Sefira is Netzah.

The Air signs are Gemini, Libra and Aquarius. Those born under these signs are advised to avoid relations with water signs – they would argue and fight all their lives, as would two born under wind signs, much as the winds blow in a different direction every day. They also make bad matches with earth signs, leading to a hard life.

Gemini

A person born under the sign of Gemini is graceful, quick-witted and a lover of wisdom, with a clever tongue. These individuals make good traders as well as teachers, are capable of capturing others' attention and expressing themselves clearly. Men and women both are talkative and of great intelligence, but can also be restless and slightly unsteady. They are adaptable and don't tend to excite, rarely stick to a goal, enjoy being surprising and are often on the move. They are associated with Mercury, their Sefira is Tif'Eret, and their sign is the sign of the shoulders and the nervous system.

Libra

Under the sign of Libra are men who are fertile and women who bear many children, though they tend to be sickly. They may be cowardly or easily given to disagreement and strife, but are basically kindly and just. Men keep themselves balanced, value justice, goodness and the arts, and their company is very pleasant as they are modest and considerate. They sometimes look sloppy and, in the way of artists, are not very practical-minded, but they can be successful diplomats. Women are beautiful and radiate grace and warmth. They have bright, joyful eyes and bring their husbands good fortune. Their planet is Venus, their Sefira, Chesed and their sign is tied to the hips.

Aquarius

Aquarius is the sign of kindly people who give help to all who ask, sometimes at great risk to themselves, even to the point of imprisonment. They tend to be unusual. Men are secretive and informal, self-sacrificing, sensitive, respectful and considerate. They have vision and faith, but are also easily influenced and excitable, if not gullible in negotiations. Women make their living easily, have a strong voice and great charisma, but tend to be cold. Their planet is Saturn, their sign oversees the legs and the bloodstream, and their Sefira is Hod.

The water signs are Cancer, Scorpio and Pisces. They make excellent matches with earth signs, since the mingling of water and earth is the symbol and beginning of all fertility, leading to success, a good family and great wealth. Two water signs would be equal in all things – if one loves fiercely, the other would return his or her love, though it would be much the same with hate.

Cancer

Cancer is the sign of people who are wise but quick to anger, at times lazy, given to moods and deep-running emotions, nostalgic to a fault and ill-tolerant of change. They are tied to their home and their family and go to great lengths to make their loved ones happy. Through being kind and helpful to all they overcome negative impulses and emerge from disagreements with the upper hand. They tend to be well-organized. Women are beautiful, shy and feminine, quick to find love, and are the subject of envy of man. They are influenced by the moon and their sign represents the chest and stomach, their Sefira is Netzah.

Scorpio

Those born under Scorpio are quarrelers and easily upset. In their lives, at first they suffer loss, then gain great wealth and joy. They are suspicious at times and jealous of their honor. Men enjoy great control and are careful and reliable, but may not choose their friends well. They can be vengeful and cruel and are willing to lie to achieve their goals; they can be very lustful, but also brave and spiritual. Women are miserly with their wealth but kind with words and have a captivating voice and gaze. Their planet is Mars, their Sefira is Gevurah and the part of the body linked to their sign is the genitalia.

Pisces

Those born under Pisces are just, reliable, honest, helpful, eager to please all and ease anyone's suffering. They are modest and adaptable, keep away from evil, and love life and art. If not caught by hesitation and sacrifice, they soon gain great honor and glory, are lucky, and in old age are surrounded by family and wealth. Women are sensual and dark eyed, require unique attention and love, have great strength of will and a love of order. Their planet is Jupiter and their Sefira is Yesod. Pisces stands for the feet.

A Dictionary of Terms, Practices and Applications

Animals

God created many kinds of animals in his world, and they are all for the benefit of mankind. No animal is there that cannot be used by man, from the smallest to the greatest.

These are the ways of animals: They were born with the knowledge of what saves them from predators or poisonous foods. Dogs eat a certain weed that causes them to vomit if they eat something dangerous, and when a rooster fights a snake, it eats a weed that saves it from its venom. If an elephant is hunted, it flees into the water and splashes the hunter with its trunk until he turns away. When birds fight, they place a healing plant on their wounds, and they know how to build their nests so they are both strong and soft. Bees also build their honeycombs in such a way as to hold the most honey within, and spiders know how to make a web to catch their food. As there are cruel and gentle people, so there are cruel animals and gentle animals.

Bat: The bat has many merits - one of them is improving memory. If a person carries its tongue on his body, his enemies would not reign over him.

Camel: The camel eats once every three days and can go without drinking for eight. It lives thirty years, and it is said that camel males cannot tell each other apart from females until they mate. While they mate they become angry and would kill any man or animal that observes them. There is a star, called "the star that kills camels", which, if a camel sees it, would die at once. A camel's wool, plucked from its neck, can help children stop wetting their bed if tied on their left hands while they sleep.

Cat: A black cat's heart tied inside a bear's skin is said to have mystic qualities that make a person invisible.

Chicken: If a rooster's head is put on an ant hill and left until the ants eat away all its flesh, a gem would be revealed in its skull. Whoever carries it would find all he seeks or receive all he asks of other men. A hen's brain put over a snake's bite would provide protection from the venom, and a rooster's burned droppings would cure one who drank poison.

Crab: The mix of a live crab ground down with donkey's milk helps against snakebites and scorpion stings. Their juices are good against snoring.

Crocodile: There is in its head a stone that is good against all poisons and venom. A man who carries it would triumph over all his enemies.

Crow: If you bury a crow's heart at a crossroad and return after thirty days, you would find there a weed. If you take the weed and bury if for thirty more days, then take it and go back to your house, you would meet a man on the way who would tell you that he wants the weed. Tell him then that if you give him the weed, he should give you the stone. Then take the stone and witness the wonders it would bring.

Deer: A belt of the skin of a deer or elk cures and wards off any plague. If one burns the horns of a deer within the house, all harmful creatures such as snakes and scorpions would flee.

Dog: A woman in hard labor would give birth at once if she drinks a she-dog's milk mixed with water, which is also good remedy for a woman wanting to miscarry.

No dog will ever bark at one who carries a black dog's tooth on him. If a man is bitten by a dog, he should also carry on him a dog's tooth, as should a child whose teeth did not yet fall. To take revenge upon one's enemy, take the right eye of a black dog and bury it in the enemy's house and one would see vengeance done.

Donkey: The fried liver of a donkey helps epileptic people, as may its hooves, if ground to powder or carried on the body.

Eagle: An eagle's eye bound in a wolf's skin and passed over the eyes guards from any ill, and its heart in a deer's skin guards from demons and harmful spirits. Its tongue placed in the right shoe would bring one great honor even from one's enemy. An eagle's gall mixed with garlic juice, fat, honey and spit cures any disease in a body it is smeared on. A paste from its dried and ground kidneys, sulfur and sesame cures leprosy. To strengthen a man's sexual prowess, mix the kidneys with cooked eggs and drink. If you tie the feather of an eagle on the left thigh of a woman in labor, she would give birth swiftly and smoothly.

Fish: There are types of great fish that have three or four great white stones in their heads. These are good for curing kidney stones and for those who cannot pass urine. A fish's gall, if put in an eye, would clear and heal it, and the smoke of a burned fish's heart banishes any demon or ghost that might come in a person.

Fox: The fox's pelt is good for pregnancy.

Frog: If cooked in water, salt and oil, it and its juices are good for healing snakebites, even venomous ones. The ashes of a burned frog stop all bleeding.

Goat: The smoke of a burned horn of goat would help a woman in difficult labor, and if you take the ashes, put them inside a cloth and place them by a sick man's head, it would help him fall asleep. The water that drips from a goat's liver when fried can improve one's night vision, and the smoke also has great merits.

Hoopoe: A creature of many merits. If you put the dry bones of a hoopoe in a glass of water, whoever touches the first bone that floats would love you fiercely. Burn a hoopoe's heart on a fire – if the smoke comes up rolling in rings, it will fulfill your every wish.

Horse: It is told of horses that, although more filled with lust than any animal, they would not mount their mother. A horse which did so unknowingly, led to her with its eyes covered, threw itself off a cliff and died. The ashes of its hooves, if mixed with vinegar, make a good remedy for a man bitten by any animal.

Hyena: When this fearful beast sees a man, it stands up on its two rear legs, strikes its belly with its two hands making sounds like a great drum, and laughs till the man laughs with it. When he laughs, the hyena steals all sense and thought from him, and he follows it to its den, where it cracks open his skull and eats his brain while the rest it leaves whole. If others see the crazed man and chase him and draw his blood, he at once regains his senses, and the animal flees.

Lion: Even a person as brave as a lion should be humble and know fear. It does ill to a person to fear nothing

Lizard: A live lizard ground down without cooking might help a man stung by a scorpion if put on the sting.

Monkey: An animal much like a human. If you cannot sleep, take some of its hair, put it under your pillow and you would fall asleep at once.

Mouse: If you burn the tail of a dead mouse covered in clay and throw its ashes in an enemy's house, vengeance would be done on them. If you put a live mouse on a scorpion's sting, it would be healed.

Ostrich: The ostrich does not sit on its eggs. Those who eat them die in a plague; these animals are poisonous.

Owl: There are several types of owls. One lives in the mountains and inside of it there is a stone that causes vomiting if put under the tongue on the first or last day of a moon's cycle. The second comes from India, and inside it is a stone that can foretell the future if put under a man's tongue.

Ox: If you put its hair in the drink of one you desire, they will soon come to you.

Pig: A deaf man would hear if some gall of pig mixed with a woman's milk would be put in his ear. To stop bleeding, one puts the ashes from burned pig dung on the wound. The pig's blood can help a woman make her breasts become smaller.

Pigeon: Dried pigeon droppings turned to ash in an oven and mixed with a newly laid egg, are a cure for hernia. To ensure that friends or lovers would never part, take a male pigeon's liver and burn it to ash inside a pot of clay, which must not touch the ground. Bake the ashes into a cake. If any of the two should eat this, they will never be parted.

Rabbit: If you put the tongue of a rabbit under your own and kiss the one you desire, he or she would be yours. A rabbit's dung hung around a woman's neck would prevent pregnancy while its stomach would encourage it. Take that stomach and wash it perfectly clean, then take a shovel that has not yet been worked with, heat it on a fire and place the stomach on it till it burns to ashes. These ashes the man and his wife should swallow or drink with water before lying together for three nights, after which the woman will conceive.

Rat: The blood of a rat is a good remedy for aching joints if placed on them. If burned while alive and its innards them extracted, salted and left to dry in the shade, a rat's body becomes a cure for the bite of all deadly venomous creatures. Ground to powder and mixed with wine to drink, the body is cured of all seizures and fits. If you put a rat's tongue in your left shoe, no enemies of yours could speak while facing you.

Skink: Burned down to ash, stops any bleeding from any place in the body.

Snail: If you cover its antennae with wax, put them in your mouth and then kiss the one you desire, they will love you fiercely.

Snake: Even if its body is cut to pieces, it lives on, and can be killed only by smashing its head. It has many merits.

Sparrow: There are two stones in its stomach, one black and one greenish. The green stone can be bound in the skin of a calf or an elk, and that is a remedy for healing old pains. A person who carries the stone, it is said, would win others' favor. The black stone is good for curing fever and sicknesses caused by dampness, and against an angry heart. If washed in water, the water would heal all diseases of the eye, as might eating the birds' flesh.

Turtle: One who carries its bony armor can become invisible. The turtle has two stones in its head - one reddish and one black. If taken out while it still lives, they would have in their centers green shapes like an eye or a frog. If swallowed, one such stone causes vomiting and the clearing and purifying of the stomach. If both stones are held together over a limb touched by venom, they would change their color and burn the hand that holds them to show proof of the venom's presence.

Wolf: The bone of a wolf's tail, its eyes and its teeth are good for preventing seizures in children. If one hangs a wolf's tail in his house, flies would not come in. If a wolf's skin is burned inside, the smoke chases away all mice and rats. Wolf's milk put on a woman's throat while asleep would cause her to voice her every thought. A wolf's tooth hung on a horse's neck causes it to go astray, and the dried right eye of a wolf protects one who holds it from all spells and misfortune.

Ants

A sure way to be rid of a nest of ants is to put in and around it ants from another nest. When mingling together they would kill each other.

Asthma

For an asthma attack, drink warm cow's milk with butter or goat's milk straightway after milking.

Another remedy – mix honey with butter and fly, then mix into it good wine, and place the mixture in a cool place until it becomes solid. Then eat three teaspoons full of it a day. And a third remedy – a glass of oats with three glasses of water should be cooked well until but a quarter remains, then filter the water and mix it with a spoon of honey and warm it over a fire. Of this drink a spoonful every hour.

And a fourth remedy – put your hands up to your elbows in water as hot as you can bear.

Back

There are several remedies for backaches, including oils, pastes, types of compresses and baths that ease the pain. One such remedy is to lie on one's stomach on a small bag filled with warm sand.

Another is to wash the back with a stiff drink mixed with Turkish pepper several times a day.

And a third – sit for half an hour in a warm bath with much salt in the water.

Bad breath

Chewing rosemary leaves first thing after rising in the morning sweetens the breath, as does drinking water in which linen seeds were cooked. And another remedy – eat a slice of garlic, than drink a glass of wine, for thirty days. Some say that putting gold within one's mouth takes the bad smell away. To prevent bad breath, one should never eat food that fell on the ground, nor eat when one's stomach is already full of lust and not hunger .Also advised is, after eating dinner, to take a walk before going to sleep.

Barren Woman

There are, it is said, twelve things that might stop a woman from becoming pregnant.

One, that she suffers a strong headache while lying with her husband, then she should cover her vagina and her husband his penis with crow's gall before lying together.

Two, that her body makes a noise during the act, then she and her husband should cover themselves with sesame oil.

Three, if she feels pain in her womb, she and her husband should cover themselves during the act with a mixture of pepper, cumin and mustard oil.

Four, if during the act she feels a pain in her chest, they should both cover themselves with the gall of a black hen.

Five, if she feels heat in her womb, they should be covered in phosphor.

Six, if her feet ache during the act, she should mix linen seed and egg yolk in butter and honey and put that in wool, then carry the wool in her womb for three days.

Seven, if the woman's heart and spine ache, meaning a coolness in her womb, she should grind myrtle and citron leaves well, mix with honey and carry the mixture in her womb for three days.

Eight, if during the act her hips and innards ache, she should put dates and lettuce in water then drink the water for three days.

Nine, if the woman sleeps after the act and does not rise, she should carry the guts and gall of a rabbit in her womb for three days.

Ten, if the woman's womb oozes a green discharge and her head aches during the act, she should carry in her womb for three days ground pomegranate.

Eleven, if she sneezes incessantly while lying with her husband and has a bitter taste in her mouth, she should cook roots with pomegranate juice and put that in her womb for three days.

And last, if the woman is under a spell, she should take oil from seven houses where no barren woman nor man are found, and leaves from seven fruit-bearing trees. These she should grind and mix and lay under the stars, then cover her body with the mix for three days.

The milk of a she-dog mixed with the milk of a she-bear, put on the stomach over the womb for three days would help a barren woman become pregnant. Or else she should take the stomach of a rabbit and a fish found inside another fish, fry them together in a pan and grind them to dust. Then mix this with flour and water and drink the mix for eight days, both morning and evening.

Another few remedies – powder from a ground ruby or from the dried womb of a rabbit mixed with wine and drank by man and wife both before lying together. Or to breathe the steam from water in which rosemary is boiled, or put the brain of a pigeon on her womb all day before lying with her husband, or sesame and the blood of a black hen. Or lastly, to dry and grind a crow's tongue and gall and drink the powder with wine.

A woman who was never able to become pregnant should cook a sheep's liver and lung in fine old wine, then lay the pot on the floor in a hot closed room, and stand over it so the steam would come into her. When the pot begins to cool, she should go to her bed and take care to remain warm until her husband comes.

This is a miraculous remedy for a barren woman: at the beginning of her period she should keep three stains of blood, one each day, and when her period is done she should keep her urine for three days also. On the third day, she should go with another woman to a place where fruit-bearing trees grow. She should be silent walking and silent returning, telling the secret of her deed to none. Then she should pick for herself a tree she recognizes, and standing before it, say this: "Tree, tree, I come to you a barren woman and now I take your pregnancy and your fruit and leave you my barren stock. That I should be fruitful and fresh and bear fruit and child, and you would be dry and bare in my place."

Then she should make three cuts in the tree and in each one put some of her period's blood from one day, and repeat the words she spoke. Then she should cut in half three fruits, if ones grow on the tree. At last she should dig a ditch by the roots and water the tree with her urine. Then, before she lies with her husband, she should eat of the fruit of the tree, and she will become pregnant. This remedy was tested and proven true several times.

If a woman has already become pregnant once and wishes to bear a child again, she should do one of two things. One is to sit on a chair on which a pregnant woman sat with no clothes on her body, for at least half an hour. The second is to dry a fish that was found inside another fish and the stomach of a rabbit, grind them to thin powder and drink it with water.

When a man and his wife fight often, it can lead to the woman becoming barren, a harmed sheep as she is called, and she would not become pregnant until doing this: to gather the blood from her period in a bowl of wax, then seal the bowl and bury it under an apple tree. Then she would bear child, and the tree would become barren.

If it is the man who is barren and not his wife, he should eat two skins of ducks before lying with her, or else, to burn an ox's ligament, mix the ashes with wine and drink it. Otherwise, he may cook grass in wine, and later drink that wine while hot before coming to the bed.

Bees

For the sting of a bee or fly there is one remedy – catching the stinger and smearing it over its sting.

Birth

When about to give birth, the woman should do the following to ensure a smooth, swift birth - First she should put a needle by a lamp that is by her bed to guard her from Lilith, the woman-demon. Second, she should ensure that her other children are not in the house. She should place her bed so that it does not face westwards or southwards, and she should wash herself in wine.

If the labor is difficult and going badly, a remedy for the woman is to take pieces from a donkey's hooves and burn them inside a bowl between her legs so that the smoke would enter her body and she would give birth at once. Or else, she should drink date pits ground and mixed with wine, or the ashes of a small frog mixed with wine, or dried horse dung with water or wine, without knowing what it is she is drinking. Also she may drink a she-dog's milk with water, or the milk of another woman mixed with egg yolk every quarter of an hour, or water mixed with ground linen seed. And a last remedy – that the woman's husband should urinate within his shoe and let his wife drink a single glass of the urine.

If the woman is in pain, she may take dried fig leaves, grind them and drink them with wine to ensure a swift, painless birth. Another remedy for birthing pain is to spread the gall of a black hen on the woman's navel. A third remedy is to tie an eagle's feather on her left thigh and she would give birth at once. And a fourth, to take a ram's horn and burn it by her head so that the smoke envelops her.

If the woman has difficulty in passing the afterbirth, she should take cat's dung or a cat's tail and burn it next to her bed, so that the smoke comes upon her, and she would pass the afterbirth at once.

Blood

One whose nose has a tendency to bleed should often smell myrtle. To heal one who spits or urinates blood, they should drink almond oil every day. Or else they should take the shells of eggs that a chicken laid that very day and grind them to thin powder, then drink that powder in almond oil three times a day till they are healed. And if almonds are not to be found, they may drink it in milk or water.

For bleeding from the lungs, first call a doctor, but before that, lay the bleeding person in a bed and forbid them to talk, let them swallow small chunks of ice, and from time to time drink a spoonful of salty water and cold lemonade. Once they feel somewhat better, they should travel to a forested place where the air is clear. A second remedy for blood from the lungs is that one should drink milk with butter daily, preferably goats milk fresh from milking, and in winter drink fish oil. The person should often eat ripe grapes, and a dish that is made of legs of calves.

To stop the bleeding from circumcision, one should take the ash from burned wood and grind it further till it is made into fine powder, then sprinkle it over the cut and the blood would stop.

To stop the blood of a woman's period, she should drink several mornings, on an empty stomach, egg yolk mixed with wine or ale. Or else she should take a female frog and burn it to ash in a new pot, and put the ash in a linen packet she should wear around her neck. It is best that a woman who is healthy and pure hangs the packet around her neck. This is also a remedy for men who bleed, but for them, the frog should be a male one. Another remedy for stopping period blood is wearing the bone of a pig around one's neck.

To bring forth that same blood, the woman should grind the peels of dried almonds to powder, mix it with honey and sesame into thick dough, then cut it to pieces and fry it. This she should be eaten several times a month to begin menstruating.

Ashes of burned pig droppings or of a frog stop any bleeding from any place in the body.

Boils

This is a severe skin disease that is especially bad when infecting the scalp. One who suffers from it should cut one's hair as short as possible and use the following remedy. Take a spoonful of honey, one of frankincense and one of pig fat, one of vinegar and one of tar, cook them all together on a fire and mix well till you get a paste. Put this on the scalp for four weeks. After four weeks when the boils are healed, make a new paste of pig fat and vinegar cooked together for a long time till nothing remains of the latter. The fat that remains should be put on the scalp for four more weeks, once every night. During all that time, the hair should be cut as short as possible.

Breast Feeding

For a woman that wants her children to grow strong, she should let them suckle first from her left breast. A breastfeeding woman who wants to increase her flow of milk should eat fat and sweet foods, but avoid cooked potatoes, since these cause her milk to become thin, and salty and spicy foods, as well as onions, which cause diseases in the child. She should eat foods fried in deep oil and with a lot of sugar. Or else she should grind linen seeds into flour and mix it with honey and sesame, then flatten the dough paper-thin and fry it with some olive oil and honey. After drying, she should cut it to small pieces and eat of it several times a day, and her milk would become abundant. Or she may heat together honey, butter and grapes and eat them for nine days, or wrap her breasts with leaves of pear.

If the woman has no milk in her breasts at all, she should take the leaves of a grapevine, cook them in milk and drink the milk for three days before eating in the morning. Or else she would take seeds from dried cucumbers and drink them ground with vine, honey and oil after heating. At last, she may take a piece of the hoof of a cow's front and back right legs, burn them and drink the ashes with water. A woman who wants to stop giving milk should cover her breasts several times a day with a mixture of fresh clay and water, or dirt and olive oil.

While a woman is breastfeeding, she should avoid eating the hearts and livers of animals. She should not be nervous or angry, nor should she ever walk about with her breasts bared, for this causes the milk to be sparse and of bad quality. She should not let her child suckle after lying with her husband unless she first walks at least a mile. And lastly, if several children of the woman died in infancy, it might be that her milk is not good and she should not breastfeed the next child born.

Breasts

Garlic purifies the breasts and heals all their ailments. For pain and stiffness in a woman's breasts, cook potatoes and mash them well, then fry them with pig fat to make a paste to put on the breasts. Another paste to ease the pain is made of flour mixed with scented water, egg yolk and some sugar; put that on a bandage for the aching breasts. For another remedy, the woman should take dry droppings of pigeon that have a white color, grind them to powder, cook with the oil of linen seed, and smear the mix on her breasts.

For pain as a result of an abundance of milk, lettuce leaves help soften the breasts. If there is a wound in a woman's breast or pus in it, she should take the blood from her period and put it on her breasts, or take the fluids of hers and her husband's body after they lie together and cover her breasts with them. Or else, she should put on her breasts at night a mixture of butter, olive oil and scented water.

Burial of a pregnant woman

If a pregnant woman dies, it should at least be attempted to bury her and her unborn child separately, or else some of the men and women who bring her to be buried might be harmed. There are several ways to bring the unborn child forth from the womb without cutting the woman open. First it is customary to wait three days before the burial, with midwives trying to cause the child to be born and placing the body every day in a bath of hot water. And if that does not help, three wise men should come and warn her to give her unborn or suffer a great punishment for a great sin. They should sound the shofar before her and threaten her that if the unborn child is not given she would be buried outside the graveyard as those who take their own lives. And if, after all this, the child remains inside her, the men should tell her: "here we decree in the name of God that you should bring harm to no man or woman for being buried with the child in your womb, and our hands are clean". After all this, she and her child may be buried.

Burns

Every burn should first be cooled, and for this, put some fresh mud on it straightaway, mixed with some vinegar or cold water. Also good is to put alcohol mixed with finely ground salt on the burn. If these are not to be found, mix cold urine with egg yolk in equal measures and put cold compresses of it on the burn.

Children

Kabbala tells us many ways to ensure the birth of healthy sons or daughters, and some that keep children from dying young. One is that the father should write or print for him a Bible. And if he cannot write or print, he should buy, then lend them to others to learn from.

For a couple whose children die, the woman should take some of the seed her husband spilled as they lay together, and give but a taste of it to the child born of that union, and none of their children would again die. And this is sure only if the husband has not sinned and spilled his seed in vain after the birth of the child. For children not to die while young, their parents should give them no true name after they are born, and only name their true name when they grow into adolescence.

Sometimes it is difficult to know what bothers babies and small children who still cannot talk and complain. There may be many reasons for them to cry or refuse to eat when none outwardly appear.

For a baby that refuses to eat, one should first check its mouth and then its mother's breasts for any flaws, and if there are none, the mother should take the baby, bare of any clothes, and hold it to her until it is warmed by the heat of her body. This she should do until it agrees to suckle. It is good to keep the child warm, and sometimes helpful to put

some clear honey on the woman's breasts. Also ask if the
mother did not smell some food while carrying her child,
and if she did, one should let the baby taste of that same
foodstuff and so it would wish to suckle.

While a baby's teeth are growing, it is in great pain. To
ease that pain, warm some butter or chicken fat and soak it
into a piece of cloth, then put the cloth to the gums once or
twice a day, and also to the throat and the back of the baby's
neck, and the teeth would grow easily. Another remedy is to
hang a tooth of a horse or dog around the child's neck. For
a child that cries constantly, his parents should lay under his
head a bone that a dog spat out while eating, or lay on his
head a ram's horn, or dirt from under the family's house
mixed with milk.

Cough

A remedy for cough is a spoonful of white vaseline and
a spoonful of almond oil mixed and heated together and
rubbed into the chest in the mornings and evenings.

Crying

It does good for a baby to cry. To people less than forty
years of age, tears are harmless, but for people who are

older, tears harm the eye and may even cause blindness. Myrrh and saffron together put to a tearing eye may stop the tears.

Deafness

A remedy for one who cannot hear - take the fall of a pig and mix it with a woman's milk and put it in their ear. Or else, take the milk of a she-dog, boil it and put it in their ear.

Diarrhea

There are two types of diarrhea, one caused by cold and one caused by spoiled foods that befoul the stomach and innards. For the latter, the remedy should be one to cleanse the stomach. For the former, use remedies that warm the digestive track. Warm compresses are one such remedy. First heat dry bran and add a little vinegar to moisten it, then boil it and put it on a small sack of cloth to cover the stomach. This compress should be changed every hour or two.

Another remedy for diarrhea - eat an egg cooked in vinegar or drink wine in which pepper was cooked, and after this, linger by the table as long as possible, then go straightaway to bed, and wash after waking from sleep. Or else cook together almond milk, old cheese and myrtle leaves and eat - this is also good for stomachaches. A third remedy - take a cow's gall-bladder, tie its end close and put it inside the anus.

Chestnuts, myrtle fruits, red roses, cooked rice or rosemary fruits in white wine are all good for stopping diarrhea. If there is blood in the feces, one should dry some nut tree flowers, mix with a fried egg and eat the mixture on an empty stomach for some days.

Disease

If you mix the gall of an eagle with garlic juice, fat, honey and spittle and cover your body with it, it would cure any sickness.

A couple who have a small child who is very sick should fast each year on the day of its birth, and if they are unable to fast, each of them should give charity to the needy on this day instead. This they must do until the child is thirteen years old.

A remedy for one who is very sick - they should change their name, but only after taking sage advice.

Here is a way to know if a sick person should heal or not. First take the name of the person and of his mother and find their numerical value, and add them together with the number of days the person has been ill. Then discard the value of every third "c" letter, and examine both the result and the day the man fell sick.

If he fell sick on a Sunday or Wednesday, and the result is one – he would live, and if the result is two, he would die, and if it is three, there is some doubt. If he fell sick on a Monday or Thursday, and the result is one – there is doubt, if two remains, then he will die, and if three, then he will live. If he fell sick on a Tuesday, a Friday or a Saturday, and the result is one, then he would die, if it is two he would live and if three – there is doubt.

Dogs

One who fears dogs should carry on him the tooth of a great black dog, and none of them would bark at him. The bite of a rabid dog is very dangerous and cannot be healed by folk or Kabalistic remedies alone, but must be treated by an expert doctor. In the meantime, the bitten person should cut the wound open and let it bleed as long as possible, then tie two strings tightly one on each side of the bite. He should take an onion and crush it, mix it with salt and honey and put the paste on the bite.

Another option – if the rabid dog is killed at once, the life of the bitten person would be saved.

Dream Signs

These are the meanings of the signs that a man sees in his dreams, taken from countless debates that appear on the subject in the Kabbala.

Apples – if given to the dreamer or they eat them, they would soon become ill, and if they do not, they foretell good news.

Arrow – one who collects arrows in his dream would come to sorrow.

Bare feet – mean loss.

Bear – foretells the death of one's enemy, or a battle.

Beard – if a man sees his beard cut, it is an ill sign, and if he sees it washed, a good one.

Bees – if one is stung by bees, his enemies would hurt him.

Belt – if the dreamer wears a belt, they would see profit, and if the belt is lost, it foretells grief.

Birds – their nests are a sign of profit, but if they are made of silver or of gold, they tell of strife.

Birth – a woman giving birth foretells hardship, and if the dreamer sits on her bed, he would not find what he seeks.

Blood – bloodshed in a dream foretells sorrow.

Breasts – if full of milk to suckle, mean profit. A woman who sees her breasts cut off should expect hardship.

Bride – dreaming of being in a bride's house foretells grief.

Building – if the building is whole it is a good sign, but not so if it is ruined.

Camel – foretells goodness, but falling off a camel means torment.

Cart – foretells illness or enmity.

Cheeks – if a man is kissed on his cheek in a dream, his enemies would fall.

Chickens – a rooster means a son to be born, and a hen means many children.

Children – if they play, they foretell happiness.

Citron – a good sign.

Clothes – if a man wears white in his dream, it is good, but if his clothes are torn, it is an ill sign. If he tears his own clothes, all his sins are forgiven. If he takes them off, then if he is ill it is a good sign, and if healthy, a bad one.

Colors – are all good signs, except light blue.

Crocodile – foretells grief.

Crow – a sign of profit.

Dead – one who sees men who have died in their dream would know rest, and if they are in their house. they would know joy and profit. If they eat in their house or give them anything, it is a good sign, unless they give a lock or a sandal.

Digging – if a man is healthy, seeing himself dig is a good sign, and if he is ill, a bad one.

Dogs – if they chase the dreamer, he would have a bad name.

Donkey – one who rides a donkey in his dream would lose in business, and if he falls off the donkey he would become poor.

Door – a door falling in a dream means the death of the dreamer's wife.

Drinking – ale foretells grief, but milk or water are good signs. A bitter drink or a remedy mean loss or strife. Old wine is a sign of happiness, but new wine a sign of hardship. If a person dreams that they are drunk, they would soon fall ill.

Eating – if a man eats pork in his dream he would be rich. If vegetables, it is a sign that his wife is unfaithful, or his name would be dishonored. Grapes foretell goodness. White bread foretells prayers answered, and bread and vegetables good fortune, but bread that is not white means worry. One who eats onions or garlic would find his name cursed. If one eats the meat of deer, it is a good sign, and if the meat of ox, they would be rich, and if one eats one's own flesh, they would soon have a great task to fulfill, but roasted meat means coming loss. One who dreams themself eating, drinking then dying in their home has dreamed a good sign for them and all their family.

Eggs – if eggs in a dream are broken, a request would be fulfilled, and if they are boiled, then a prayer would be answered.

Elephant – if the dreamer rides an elephant, they would be set a task without profit.

Face – means respect gained.

Feet – if the dreamer sees their feet cut off, it foretells riches.

Filth – means a fight, or seeing something the dreamer would rather not see.

Find – whatever a person finds in their dream, if they are rich, they would become poor, and if they are poor, they would be rich.

Fire – means anger, but burning without a flame means a woman's love.

Fish – large fish mean rains, while small ones mean profit soon gained.

Forest – one who enters a forest in a dream would become a leader.

Fruits – are all good signs except dates.

Gems – if given, mean profit, and if not given, mean grief.

Glass – a good sign.

Goats – a single goat foretells a good year, many goats foretell many of these.

Gold – all gold in a dream is an ill omen.

Goose – coming wisdom.

Grapes – foretell childbirth, and dreaming of making wine foretells profit.

Grapevine – means need fulfilled, but a grapevine bearing grapes means coming mourning.

Grief – a good sign, unless the dreamer is ill.

Hair – if washed, is a good omen, and if the dreamer

sees their hair revealed, they would be soon beaten by others.

Hands – if a man's hands are cut off in a dream, it foretells riches.

High place – if a person stands on a high place, they would be loved by men of power, and if they come down from a high place, they would descend from greatness. If they look up to a high place, long life is foretold.

Hill – if a man climbs a hill, he would find fortune, and if he walks on a hill, then greatness.

Horses – mean coming strife. A black horse is an ill omen, but a horse running, or a white horse, mean profit.

Hotel – a hotel seen in a dream means profit.

House – if a house in a dream burns without smoke, it foretells a lucky find for the dreamer. Many houses foretell sorrow, but a man who dreams that his house is in ruins would win a good name, and if a stone rises from the ruins he would reach greatness.

Insects – good signs every one.

Letter – a new letter means joy.

Lightning – means profit.

Meat – a man who gives out meat in his dream would have meat on his own table.

Mice – mean change.

Myrtle – means many assets, or inheritance.

Nakedness – means poverty.

Nostrils – if they are blocked, there is one who feels no more anger towards the dreamer.

Old age – means loss in business.

Olive oil – a good sign, unless one drinks it, in which it foretells that his wife would sleep with another.

Ox – if fat and strong, foretells a good year, and if weak, foretells poverty. A running ox or one browsing in a field mean joy, but a plowing ox means mourning. If the dreamer is running from the ox, they would soon embark on a long journey. If they fall from the ox it is a bad omen, but a good one if they kill it or eat from it; if they ride it, it is a sign of respect. A white ox means the downfall of the dreamer's enemies, and one who bites the dreamer means a long life. A maiden who sees an ox in her dream would soon know torment.

Palm branch – means goodness.

Path – walking in a path is a good sign.

Pig – pigs that fight are a sign to guard oneself.

Pillar – means that the dreamer should leave their home or come to harm.

Poverty – one who dreams that they are poor, would soon become so.

Prayer – a good sign.

Rain – foretells good news.

Ring – if of silver and gold, means riches.

River – if the river is slow, it means peace, and if swift, the dreamer should beware of their enemies.

Sea – if a man falls in the sea and does not rise, it means mourning to come.

Sister – coming wisdom.

Ship – a small ship foretells heaven for the dreamer, and if they enter a ship, it means the same for their children. A ship loaded with goods is a sign of sins forgiven. Leaving a ship tells of a journey to come.

Snake – a good sign, and if it bites the dreamer then they would have a son soon, and if they kill it, then their enemies would fall before them, and if they speak to it, the great would hear their words. But if the snake is cut, it means loss, and if they run from the snake, their trade be gone from them, and if the snake chases, then their enemies are to chase them soon. If the dreamer sees a snake in his bed, he should take a wife, and if he has a wife already she would soon die.

Snow – snow and ice are signs of being saved from one's enemies.

Spear – means that the dreamer should guard themselves from harm.

Spring – washing in a spring foretells joy.

Stars – mean profit and joy.

Statues – if shaped like people, speak of love or family.

Sun and moon- foretell strife.

Tears – one who sheds tears in his dream would be happy.

Teeth – if a tooth of the dreamer falls, their son or relative would die if it is an upper tooth, or if a lower tooth, then one who loves them is destined to die.

Tools – if of silver and gold, they mean bad advice would be revealed and become harmless; musical instruments mean the dreamer would see men weep; weapons of war mean that he must not fear his enemies.

Trees – one tree tells of joy, many trees mean many children to be born. If the trees are uprooted, war is coming. One who dreams of climbing a tree would see honor and greatness, but if the tree is falling on him, ill times are at hand and the people of his home mean him harm, and he should go to another city to live to be saved.

Vineyard – foretells pregnancy for the dreamer's wife.

Walking – if a man walks to a graveyard, he would be judged and cleared. If he walks on a mountain or hill, he would become great, and if by the river or sea, he would not leave his house that day. If he sees himself walking from afar, he would soon receive a letter.

Wall – if a wall of a person's house falls in a dream, they would be rich.

Washing – in a fountain or the sea means joy, and in cold water means good news to come. Only washing in hot water is a bad sign.

Well – a sign of peace.

Wheat – means peace.

Wolf – small wolves mean rain, and large wolves mean profit.

Wool – if white, means joy.

Women – if in a man's dream he lies with his wife, a fight is foretold, and if he lies with another man's wife, then certainly heaven awaits him if only he does not lust after her. If he lies with his mother it foretells goodness, and if he lies with a young girl, then honor.

Dreams

A good dream should be told and spoken of for dreams follow the words spoken. A bad dream should be put away from one's mind and not thought of at all. The more one lingers on bad dreams, the worse they would seem.

This should a person know, to never tell their dreams to any but one who truly loves them. And witness Joseph – he told his dreams to his brothers who hated him, and thus delayed their fulfillment. Had he said nothing, his dreams would have come about at once. A person who sees in their dream another person kissing them is a bad sign, foretelling that death will come soon to a loved one.

Drinking

A drunken man wishing for sobriety should soak a rag in vinegar and wrap it around his testicles.

A drinker who wishes to break that sinful habit but finds

his will weak should drink a spoonful of good olive oil every two hours, or three spoonfuls of fish oil a day, for as long as he needs to stop drinking.

Earaches

A person whose ears ache, should fry an onion, squeeze out its juice, mix it with an equal amount of almond oil, soak a thread with it and put in his ear to sooth the pain. Another remedy - take some gall of an animal, mix some of the person's urine and some woman's milk, all in equal shares. Warm the mix a little, soak a thread in it and put it in the ear. A third - a cloth soaked with warm water in which the wood of an olive tree was cooked. And a last one - take a woman's milk and mix it with that of a she-dog and grape juice, boil some lentils in it, then put a drop of the resulting liquid in the ear.

For a child's earache - a breast-feeding woman should drip some of her milk into the child's ear. For bad hearing - take some fat from a chicken and some from a goose and melt them together, filter the mixture and cool it, put some drops in the defective ear. For ringing in the ear - boil equal parts of sheep gall and olive oil, soak a thread in it and put it in the ear. Or else, cook a citron peel in olive oil and put three drops into the ear in the morning, and three more in the evening. If a small insect enters the ear, as at times might happen, boil butter with salt and put a drop of the cooled mixture in the ear. Or else, warm some almond oil and put it in the ear.

Eating

There are ten rules for eating well that, if followed properly, ensure that eating would bring no harm and no problems or diseases to the stomach.

Never swallow the food without proper chewing.

Do not eat when angry.

Do not eat meat except in the evening.

A night meal must be lighter than a day meal.

Do not eat heavy food before light food.

Do not eat bread warm or not well baked.

Do no eat boiled egged.

Do not eat old fish or meat.

Do not eat a fruit with its peel.

Drink no stiff drinks.

Elements

The four elements of this world are Earth, Air, Fire and Water. Co-dependent and ever-changing, they make up all there is upon the world. They may join and separate and transform into one another, and are reflected in the souls of men.

Air is the element of abstract thinking, the energy that is present everywhere in the world, the spirit without which no matter may exist. It stands for wisdom, spirituality and intelligence, but also, at times, for apathy and laziness. This spirit exists also in fire and in water.

Earth represents the power of solid reality, a firm grip on what is, the physical world, common sense, coolness and clarity, responsibility. It encompasses fire's energies with it and counters its burn – mercy to its judgment, matter to its spirit. Those who come from the earth element are in this world to learn to restrain their greed for the material and bring spirit into their lives.

Fire stands for life and warmth, vividness, positive energy, power, noise and ruckus and vanity. It includes the other three elements within it – it may either feed them through use of positive energy or burn by negative energy. One whose essence is fire must be wise enough to use his passions well and not be burned. One who lives a cultured, restrained life would find it easy to balance the fire's energy. These are people who were born to learn and teach how to love and give to others.

Water is emotion and balance. Just as there is water above in the sky and rain and water below in the sea and underground, just as the water follows nature's cycle, so do those born of water have higher and lower emotional centers that must be balanced or they risk causing mental illness. Thus these individuals are introverted, sensitive, prone to moods and have been born to find control, balance and peace.

Enemy

To make an enemy of yours surrender, take mustard and salt in one vessel, pass urine into it, and put it in a hidden place for three days. Then spill some of the contents on your enemy's doorstep, and he would surrender to you.

To shut an enemy's mouth that he should not speak ill of you, take a long string of linen, go to a grave and cut of the string the grave's length from headstone to end. Then tie many knots in the string, saying with each knot: "here do I tie this man's mouth shut that he should not speak ill on me". Then, bury the string there.

To be safe from all enemies – carry in your belt a snake's head, and the eye of a rooster at your side.

When a person is in dire danger from their enemies, they should speak the following three times: "I have met with my foes and see them and they shall not see me, I will govern them and they shall not govern me. Their words are as the earth and my words over them. Theirs are the heads of asses and mine is the head of a lion. Theirs are the tongues of pigs and mine is the tongue of a king."

Epilepsy

This is a chronic disease of the brain that causes seizures, unconsciousness and foaming at the mouth. There are some remedies that can ease the disease and others that try to banish it from the sick person's body altogether.

One who is epileptic should keep himself from anger, from hearing singing voices, from going to hot springs or to funerals. They should not eat bread warm, or dark bread nor cheese or beef, or the heads of chickens or fish. They should not drink alcohol but only water that was boiled and cooled, and best the water used to cool hot iron. Each morning they should eat quickly when they leave their bed and never fast. A remedy is that they should eat nine mustard seeds every morning. Or else, they should always carry in their pocket some salt, and when they feel an attack about to happen, they should swallow some of the salt with water and thus weaken it. For an epileptic child, they should sleep with nine pieces of iron under their pillow.

One possible remedy is to let the epileptic breathe the smoke of a burning rooster's cockscomb taken swiftly after slaughtering it, or the smoke of the heart of a raw fish. It is said the disease would not remain in the body of one who eats foul things, such as the fried liver or meat of a donkey. Or else he should eat the afterbirth from a female pig's first litter or a she-cat's, dried and ground to fine powder and mixed with water or baked into a cake. Finally, a remedy is to let an ox drink from a bowl of water, and collect what drips out of its mouth and let the epileptic man drink that.

Eyes

For red and fevered eyes, mix egg yolk with fine wine, soak a cloth with it, and put it several times on the aching eye. For a sty, put a piece of bread soaked with milk on the eye. One who cannot see at all at night – this is called "rooster blindness" for they become sightless in the evening when the roosters sleep – should take the liver of an ox for a man or cow for a woman and cook it in a wide pot. Then he or she should lean over the pot with opened eyes that they be filled with steam. Then when the liver is cooked, he or she should eat it and be fully cured.

For dullness of the eyes, one can cook the flowers, fruits, leaves and bark of a peach tree together and put the liquid to the eye, or do the same with fish gall or well-cooked olive oil. This is a remedy for sickness of the eyes: take a tube made from the stalk of fennel, fill it with sugar and close its ends with wax. Then put the tube into the body of a hen that is not yet one year old and bury the hen on its feathers and the tube within it for thirty days. When the tube is taken out it has inside it a liquid that should be put in a bowl. One drop of this should be put into the eyes, once in the morning and once in the evening, till the eyes are healed.

Fasting

A great remedy for many things. One who has a small child that is very ill should fast on that child's birthday every year until he or she is thirteen years old.

Feet

Aching, weak feet should be washed with kerosene three times a week.

Fire

To protect a house against fire, a woman should hang a cloth stained with the blood of her period on the wall facing the fire. The fire would not catch on the side where the cloth hangs.

Fish

A man who eats small fish will not become sick with diseases of the stomach. Small fish are a remedy for the body.

Fleas

To be rid of fleas, put kerosene or ox gall mixed with strong vinegar in the places where they hide.

Food and Drink

Almonds: Their oil is good and they are beneficial for urinating and for the lungs. They cause sleepiness because they are very hard to digest.

Apples: A fine cure for depression. If eaten when cooked, ripe or fried an hour before the meal, they cause the digestive track to empty, but if eaten sour, they cause constipation.

Birds: Chickens are the best among birds to eat, easy to digest and causing good humors. Chicken strengthens the mind and body and thickens a man's seed. The meat of other birds, such as pigeons and turkeys, is also good. Goose meat is cruder and hard to digest. The younger the bird, the better its meat.

Brain: Not good for the stomach and a bad food.

Butter: Warm butter softens the stomach and breast and quenches hunger. It is best eaten before the meal or early in it rather than at its end.

Cabbage: Softens the stomach and makes in it a foul juice. Best avoided, except that it dispels drunkenness.

Cheese: Old cheese is very harmful to the body, hard to digest and causes kidney stones, especially if salted. Best to avoid eating such cheeses as they harm the stomach, make foul juices and ill humors. But if just a little of it is eaten after a meal, it may improve digestion. Fresh cheese is soft, when cold and wet it lowers swelling in the stomach and heals it, especially if it smells good. The best cheese is one still covered in butter.

Chestnuts: These are hard to digest and cause gases in the digestive track and a foul juice that causes constipation. But aside from that, they are a great pleasure.

Cinnamon: Causes urination and brings a woman's period, clears the lungs and helps digestion, strengthens the body and lowers swelling in the stomach.

Drink: Water is the best drink for anyone. If you want to test which of two sources of water is best, take two pieces of cloth of the same weight and soak each of them in one source, then lay them out in the sun till they dry. The cloth that dries faster is the one soaked in the better water. The water of springs is best of all.

Eggs: These are fine food, good to eat when fresh and best on the day they were laid, when they are as gold. If they are left a day they are as silver, if more they are as iron. Boiled they are good but fried in oil, less so. Eggs eaten in the morning on an empty stomach do the body well, they make labor easier, counter poisons and strengthen the heart.

Figs: Cooked figs are good for the stomach, the lungs, the liver and spleen. They are nutritious and best eaten when ripe and freshly picked. They are best eaten before a meal, since they empty the stomach and cleanse the kidneys. If too many are eaten, though, they cause thirst and skin rashes.

Fish: These are usually found in nature in cold water, but there are differences between different types of fish. When they live in dirty waters, they are bad, while those that live in rivers and in clear waters are fine. Fish of the open sea are finer even than fish of the rivers.

Garlic: Good for cleansing a woman's breasts, helps against skin diseases, increases the appetite and hunger. One who eats too much of it however may suffer in one's eyes and stomach.

Grapes: These are considered finer than other fruits, and are only good for eating when ripe, though they may cause those who eat much of them to gain weight. Grapes are good for children suffering from a fever, who may be cured by eating many grapes with bread.

Heart: Hard to cook, but if cooked well, makes for fine food.

Honey: All doctors praise eating honey as good for the brain and digestion, cleansing the blood and making the eater good tempered. It also eases tiredness, sharpens the senses and strengthens the body. Honey is best eaten in cold, wet weather, also as a cure for diseases caused by that weather, and might be harmful on hot summer days. The best honey is made in springtime and early summer, while wintertime honey is the least of them all, and summertime honey is of medium quality. The nature of honey changes according to the flowers from which the bees make it – the very best honey is golden and smells good with no trace of the smell of weeds.

Kidneys: Very hard to cook, cause foul and crude juices in the stomach.

Marrow: Easily digested and good for eating, but if too much is consumed, weakens the stomach and may cause vomiting.

Meat: There is an important difference between the meat of an old and young animal, and between meats with more and less fat. Doctors praise the meat of lamb; after that it is good to eat deer meat, and after that, the meat of sheep. Goat meat is also considered of high quality and best when fried. The meat of an ox is good for those who perform manual labor.

Melon: When cold, it is good for slacking thirst, causes urination and is quickly absorbed in the stomach, thus good when eaten before the meal with some salt. It is best to drink strong wine with it, but not after it, nor water.

Milk: In nature, milk is good, the best being milk that is none too fat and none too thin, from a cow who lives and feeds where good grass grows. Goat milk is less good than cow milk, which is also the fattest of milks, and the milk of sheep and donkeys is the thinnest and most watery. Milk is digested well and quickly, softens the stomach but often has ill effects on it. It must be kept well else it would grow sour and be very harmful.

Mustard: This is good for all diseases of the head and the brain.

Nuts: These are hard to digest and cause headaches and strain the lungs. However, they also help against worms. Newly ripe nuts should be eaten peeled and are best with sugar, to strengthen the stomach and the heart. Dry nuts work well to counter poison, and are best eaten with figs after fish.

Olives: Warm olive oil softens the stomach and is good against worms and poison.

Onions: Not good for eating, of an ill nature, good only when cooked with fat.

Peanuts: Very like almonds in nature, hard to digest, thicken a woman's milk and a man's seed and cause both to gain weight.

Rice: When cooked well, rice is good food for people who labor with their hands.

Saffron: Helps digestion and urinating and softens the stomach, makes intercourse more pleasant, strengthens the heart, helps the lungs and against poisons and brightens the face. It also brings forth a woman's period. But if too much of it is eaten, it might harm the brain and become as poison itself, to the point of being deadly. It is healthy so long as it is eaten moderately.

Spleen: Not good for eating, hard to digest and causes depression.

Tongue: Animal tongues are good for eating and are digested quickly, if not too hard and if not salted.

Vegetables: There are many types of vegetables, and healthiest among them is the horseradish, which cools the stomach and cleans the gall. It is good eaten either fresh or cooked, but might be harmful to the eyes. Its juice helps against poison.

Watermelons: These make a thick, foul juice within the stomach and cause diarrhea.

Wheat: This may cure a rabid dog's bit, if put on the wound fresh and without grinding and left there a long time.

Wine: This drink has many merits, strengthening and making one who drinks it lively and joyous, helps digestion and cleans the humors. Fine wine is not too sweet nor too dry, smells good and is clear and reddish, not too thick nor too thin, not too strong nor too weak. Another condition is that it not be newly made but very aged.

At the beginning of the meal one should eat the lighter, damper and thinner foods that are easily swallowed and digested. Then the heavier, drier and less easily digested foods should be eaten. Last should be the most difficult foods to digest, because if one eats the harder foods first, they would linger too long in the stomach and spoil. If one eats the lighter foods first, they would quickly make way for the heavier ones that take longer to digest.

Gems

There are some gems of great merit. One is cat's eye, which according to the wise men of India guards its wearer that they should be closer to wealth and never to poverty. Another such stone is the coral, which, when worn, guards against sickness and foretells a bright future.

Gold

This is the secret of turning copper to gold. Take nine eggs, bury them in a pot and cover them well, then put them under a mound of garbage for thirty days or more. Then crack open the eggs and you would find in each one a worm. Put everything back inside the pot and cover it, the worms will grow and eat each other until only one large worm is left. Burn it in a pot, and stand aside while it burns for the smoke is a deathly poison. Keep the ashes that remain – if you take some pure copper and melt it, and put in the melting metal some of the ash, it would turn to gold.

Head

There are seven types of headaches, counted as such:

From the stomach, ill and foul vapors rise into the neck and the head.

From warmth of the body caused by some sickness.

From cold.

From some disease of the nerves.

From the presence of too much blood, so that the heart fills the head with blood.

A headache caused not by the body but by a blow or a migraine.

To heal a headache, one should first find its cause. For a headache caused by warmth of the body, a good remedy is cold compresses of water and vinegar put on the head, or water in which two mint herbs were cooked. For a headache caused by cold, hot compresses of oats cooked in vinegar should be put on the head till sweat breaks. Sometimes a headache is eased by washing the feet up to the knee for half an hour with hot water, salt and ash.

Heart

One who suffers from weakness of the heart should eat the first thing when they rise in the morning, before doing anything else. Roses of all sorts ease the heart as they make a person merry. Nuts and cumin are good cures for illnesses of the heart.

Hernia

Cooked pears or fresh myrtle fruits are a remedy for this.

Holy Names

Those who invoke the holy names in vain or for ill purpose would be cast from this world and destroyed. They would die or fall to poverty, and if not them, then their descendants, and their punishment in hell would be very lengthy and great.

House

Kabalistic lore tells us that when a new house is built on a place where a house has never stood before, it is most vulnerable to attack by evil forces angered at the space taken from them. Therefore there are several ways to guard the new house. One is to leave an uncolored space, a foot wide and a foot high, on the house's walls. Another is to celebrate the move to a new house with a feast, invite all the poor and the needy, and sing songs to bless the new house. Or else, one can slaughter a rooster and hen in the new house and give the meat to the poor.

One who wants to move from a new house back into the

old one must wait for seven years. If for some reason they can't wait, they should leave a rooster and hen alone in the empty old house for a day and a night. Afterwards they should go and dwell there and leave them in the house for another week, then slaughter them and give their meat to four good men who are needy, and no ill shall come to them.

Impotence

An impotent man should wash his flesh in cold water every morning, fifty or sixty times. Or else he should fry some onions and squeeze the juice from them with a clean cloth, then mix with twice as much water and honey and cook over a fire, and drink before lying with his wife. A third remedy - take the ligament from the leg of a bull or a goat, dry it well and grind it to powder. Then mix that powder in a glass of wine and drink it in the morning on an empty stomach, and then in the evening, two hours before intercourse. A fourth remedy calls for the might of falling rain to drive away a man's weakness. The man should drink rainwater, or else stand in a hidden place naked and let the rain wash over his body, and also open his mouth and let the rain flow inside and wash his body from within, and this would cure many weaknesses.

Another cure is to take the brain of a crow or some ants, fry them in olive oil and put the oil on the man's penis, or do the same with nutmeg, cinnamon and ginger mixed with honey, or fried radish seed, or to drink powder from a ram's horn in wine There are a number of foods that can cure an impotent man, and some that can worsen his condition. Among the first are counted rooster meat, peanuts, meat without its fat, white wine and best when warm, cumin and honey, humus seeds in wine or water, and turnip seed with egg yolk. Of the latter are counted spices, vegetables, fish, goat meat, beef and goose, watermelons, pumpkins of all sorts, onions and cucumbers.

Jaundice

This is a serious illness that damages the liver and blood. One of its symptoms is a yellow color appearing in the eye. One remedy for this illness is to soak a sponge in the milk of a cow, warm and freshly milked, and wash the sick man's body with it. Or else, mix five drops of lavender oil with wine and drink it in the morning on an empty stomach, and to repeat this for some weeks. Another remedy - buy a brand new bowl and let the sick person urinate in it. Then put some wax in it as well and cook it on an open fire. The one who is sick should then take the bowl and leave it at a crossroads outside of town and go back home not looking once behind him.

And a third remedy - let the sick man urinate in a clean bowl and take the urine at once, mix it with flour and bake three breads, all without his knowledge. These cakes he should eat to be healed.

And finally, take a pigeon, male for a man and female for a woman, and lay it on the stomach of the one who fell sick. The pigeon will take into itself the disease, and die in his or her stead.

Jealousy

If one of a married two is exceedingly jealous of the other for no reason, his or her love should give him a drink of some dirt taken from a sparrow's nest mixed with water, and that would remove the jealousy at once.

Kidney stones

An offered cure is to take a goat and not milk it for three days and nights, then milk and drink its milk at once. Or else, to leave a clove of garlic in a glass of wine for a full day, then eat the garlic and drink the wine, this three times a day. And a third - grind seven fresh nuts with their peels and mix with cypress fruit and honey in a bowl of glass or clay. Do this in the evening, then drink the result in the morning. Other remedies include water in which oats and lettuce were cooked, the resin from a willow tree gathered in the seventh month or that of the poplar gathered in the fifth, the urine of a black goat that drank good wine, and peach tree resin mixed with red wine.

If the kidney stone is extracted with the urine, wash it and grind it, mix the powder in water and drink to prevent new stones from forming. If kidney stones cause difficulties in passing urine, cook parsley in water and drink. Another cure is to bathe in water in which barley or straw was boiled. For a small stone that is stuck in the man's penis, the organ should be washed with hot water and oil, or in water in which mouse droppings or ox gall were cooked for three days. Else the man should lie on his back and hold up his hands until the stone falls, or cover his armpits with a rabbit's fat, or eat in the morning sugar mixed with eggshell ground to powder.

Knowledge

There are ways for a person to discover hidden knowledge, such as the gender of his child, the face of his wife to be or the fate of his sick body. To know who is infertile in a couple, the man or his wife, two bowls should be filled with bran. The man will urinate in one and his wife in the other, and they would put both bowls under their bed for three days. After that, the bowl in which there are worms is that of the one who is infertile.

To know if a woman bears a son or daughter, in the ninth month she should put some of her milk in a jug of water. If it sinks, she would birth a son, and if it floats, a daughter. Another way to know is for the husband to suddenly ask his wife to show him her hands. If she shows them with their palms up, she bears a daughter, and if her palms are down, a son.

For a man to know the face of his destined wife, he should take an egg laid on Monday or Wednesday, fry it well and cut it in half. He should then eat one half before he goes to sleep and put the other under his pillow, and his wife's face would be revealed in a dream.

To know if a husband who left his wife would return, and if soon – one should add the numerical value of the woman and the day in the week in which one was asked the question, minus seven. If the result is one, he would never return. If it is two he would return. If three, he would return gladly, and if four then only after a long while. If five, he would die returning or return suffering great agonies. If six he would return soon, and if seven – never. This should also be done to know if a woman who left her husband would return.

To know if a sick man would live or die, it is said to take a piece of pig's fat, from a male for a man and female for a woman, and smear the fat on the sick man or woman's feet. The rest one should give to a dog to eat, and if the dog eats it, the sickness would be healed.

To know where in a river a drowned man's body lies, take a whole loaf of bread or a bowl of wood and put it in the water. It would at once float to and remain where the body may be found.

Ligaments

Rosemary flowers are a cure for weakness of the ligaments, as is linen oil which softens stiff ligaments, and the oil of nuts and bitter almonds. The powder of birch branches or bark cures all their ills.

Liver

The citron fruit is good for cooling the liver, as are sour pomegranates.

Loneliness

Going alone at times is a great remedy for a person's mind, it is good that sometimes a person should retreat from all things and turn to God alone. The more they turn to God, the more they are cleansed of all their sins. If a person comes alone to a field and prays there to God, every bush and tree, weed and grass in the field adds their voices to his prayer and strengthens him and it.

Loss

For finding a thing that was lost, a person should be silent and tell no other of it. They should turn their clothes inside out and wear them at times, three times in all, and then would find what was lost or have it returned. But if they tell another soul, this remedy would not work.

Love

There are many ways to cause another to love you, some for love between man and wife, some to soothe anger between them, and some for a peaceful home.

To win another's love, take a glass of water, wine or ale, fill your mouth with the drink then return it to the glass three times, then let the one you desire drink. Otherwise, mix twelve drops of urine in the glass and give it to one you desire, or the same with ox hair.

The stomach of a sparrow contains two small stones. One is red, and the other is black, and that one awakens love in the heart of one whose clothes it touches.

If a couple's love has faded with time, they should take the eye of a rabbit and a small fish, wrap them in linen, then tie the cloth closed and step on the tie.

For love between man and wife, the man should take an orange with juice as red as blood, and drop into it three drops of the blood drawn from his little finger, and give it to his wife to eat. Another remedy - the man should cut the fingernails of his hands and feet both, burn them to ashes and mix them with a drink to give his wife. A third - the man should take three hairs from the woman's head, tie them around a needle and stick the needle in the ground, or stick them in the trunk of a tree around which he should walk three times.

For a woman to gain or regain her husband's love – she should gather her sweat into a glass while sitting in a hot bath, and mix the sweat with wine for him to drink. A second advice - the woman should take nineteen whole peppers, some lime and some salt, and put it all in a bowl of clay. Then she should pour on it ale, put it on the oven and light the mix, saying: "as this burns, so would my husband's heart burn till he comes to me and do as I wish."

For household peace – the woman should write her name and her husband's on smooth parchment in one line, and under the line write "you are at peace, and your house is at peace, and all that you have is at peace". She should then put the parchment in a drink until the writing is erased, and without her husband's knowledge give that drink to him. It is best that this she does this in the glass of wine for Kiddush.

These are the spells that can be made to restore a man's love for his wife or a woman's love for her husband, and even for turning an enemy's hate into love.

If a man loves his wife no longer, she should take a handful of well-ground salt, some lime ground to powder, nineteen black peppers and some quicksilver. All this she should put in a bowl of clay and on it pour some wine. This she would put inside an oven on a Thursday morning, when all others in the house are still asleep. When the contents of the bowl start burning, she should say a prayer for her husband's love.

To restore a woman's love for her husband, he should take a hair of hers, some salt and some silver, put all this in a rag, and put the rag on hot coals inside a bowl of clay. Then when it burns he should say: "As this silver burns on those coals, so would my wife's heart burn with great love for her husband. She shall not rest and shall not sleep and shall not eat nor drink till she loves me greatly, truly, and forever, Amen Sela."

To turn an enemy's hate to love, go before sunrise outside of town and turn facing east to the sunrise. Then when the sun rises and is seen, say: "I greet you in the name of the Lord, who made me and you, and request that you should be sent before him, that he should turn his heart to love me and do as I will, and as you warm the mountains and the hills, so would you warm his heart and soul and flesh that he should love me greatly. Amen Sela." And this you should say nine times.

Lungs

For healing all diseases of the lungs, a person should eat fat foods, drink milk with butter and every day eat beef with its fat. If he cannot stomach beef he should eat calf, and if he cannot stomach that he should eat fat that is easier to digest, such as fish oil or goose, and drink hot milk every morning.

Lupine

The flour of this plant mixed with vinegar and honey is good for curing all bruises and cracks in the skin, and kills head lice.

Madness

Here is a remedy for one who has gone mad – take him and stand him under a hazel tree and cut his hair and the nails of his hands and feet. Then make a hole in the tree and put the hairs and nails inside it. Then seal the hole with a chunk of wood and say, "here is your share, and as the hairs and nails will never return to this man, so will this sickness never return to this man". Then cover his eyes so he will not see the tree, and take him back to his home. Another remedy – let the madman eat the meat of a chicken that died of no cause.

Malaria

The best cure for this disease is quinine. Take it for three days, and you will be healed. A different remedy is to take the sick person's fingernails from both hands and feet and bake them in a small cake. Then another person should take the cake to the market, speaking to no one on his way, and give it to the first dog he sees to eat. When the cake is eaten, the sick person would heal.

Or else take those same nails and put them on burning embers in a bowl with some sulfur, and the sick person should, on an empty stomach, breath in the smoke, covering his head to keep it around him. After this he should urinate on the embers and throw them away.

And a third – take a living crab, and put it in a small pouch with the sick man's nails, and the man should wear this pouch on his body and put it by his heart.

Man and Wife

When a man wishes to lie with his wife, these are some rules that he should keep, for the sake of himself, his wife and the child that might be born in the union. The first is not to indulge in the act too often, since it inflicts the spirit; a tale was told of a man who spent all his seed lying often with his wife, and became weak and sickly and inflicted with trembling in all his limbs.

Secondly, a man should not kiss his wife's pubes during the act, so the child would not be mute.

Third, the couple should not talk, so the child would not be deaf.

Fourth is not to lie together in a bed where a baby sleeps, nor lie together by moonlight or candlelight so the children would not become epileptic.

Fifth, a man should never lie with his wife while she is during her period to avoid bringing sickness upon his children.

Sixth, if a man dreams of a woman and awakens lustful, he should not lie then with his wife, for the child would have Satan's mark upon him.

Seventh, a man should not look at his wife's pubes during the act or the child would be blind.

While lying together, the man and his wife should banish every wicked thought from their hearts and think only of good and fair things, to save the child that may be conceived from being punished for his parents' sins. The purer the act is, the happier would be the child's life.

Mandrakes

Some say that mandrakes are a way to ensure fertility.

Marriage

Even if a man has several sons, he should not stay unwed without a wife.

No man is whole if alone.

It is a good deed for a man to bring others together and make matches, and an honored way to make one's living.

Mating

If a woman lies on her right side while she lies with her husband or after it, she would give birth to a son. If she lies on her left side, she would give birth to a daughter. If a man lies with his wife in a banquet or ball, in the evening hours, the child born would seek the company of its own sex – a son would desire to lie with other men and a daughter would be inclined to prefer other women - this, like the evening that is half day and half night. And this child's soul would in the end be reborn in a rabbit.

Memory

To sharpen one's memory, eat every morning on an empty stomach a taste of a spoonful of honey.

Names

There are people who customarily name their children after all sorts of animals, saying they would thus be safe from many kinds of harm. Thus are men named Wolf, or women named Cat.

Negotiations

If you put pig's lard on your leg when negotiating, you would be able to sell anything you wish.

Oaths

Taking oaths is an ill thing – if a man swears an oath and lingers in fulfilling it, a disaster may befall him, that his wife or child might die, or he might be lost at sea. Those who take oaths commit a sin.

A man is held to his oath if he is eighteen years and one month of age. A woman's oath holds if she is seventeen years and one day old.

Oils

Bitter almond oil: Opens the digestive track, lowers swelling of the abdomen and soothes gases, helpful for earaches and clears stains on the skin of the face.

Egg oil: Produced from yolk, it softens the skin and purifies it, good for cuts in the lips, hands, feet and eyelids, and infections of the ear.

Fish oil: Good against any ailment there is and gives strength.

Jasmine oil: Replenishes a man's seed, clears the throat and voice.

Linen oil: Softens stiff ligaments and helps in diseases of the anus.

Meat oil: Quells appetite, hard to digest, causes boredom and darkens a man's thoughts.

Mustard oil: Mustard cures pain that is caused by cold and helps men sleep well. Also strengthens the memory.

Nut oil: Helpful for the ligaments, cures rashes and gases.

Pumpkin oil: Good for the kidneys and against rashes, the blood and seed, lessens sexual attraction.

Saffron oil: Heals diseases of the ligaments and gives them litheness and strength, good for diseases and pains of the womb, and lends a healthy look.

Sweet almond oil: Moistens a dry throat, chest and lungs, makes a man's seed plentiful.

Old Age

A man must pray that when he is old he can see with his eyes and eat with his mouth and walk with his feet. For when a man grows old, all turn away from him and leave him alone to fill all his needs.

Clear evidence that God favors the old is that He gave them long life, and thus they should be respected. One should give utmost respect to the old, be they the plainest of men, be they women also, and this not only to the old, but to every man and woman who is wise. One must rise before any man and woman who is over sixty years old. Age has several merits, and they are wisdom, intelligence and glory.

Plague

In time of plague, one should guard oneself from cold and foul air and not go to damp places, and if the air is cold, keep one's legs and stomach warm with soft flannel cloth. Also one should not drink stiff drinks nor labor physically and mentally, be sure to eat breakfast and during the day not eat one's fill but only almost.

One should keep one's house clean and especially the bathrooms, spilling there lime every day and also vinegar. It is good to burn scented herbs in the house, or heat an iron till it is white-hot and on it pour vinegar or wine every morning and let the people of the house smell the smoke.

One should take care not to drink cold water, but to boil the water first and drink it warm and best with tea or mint leaves. One should not eat fresh fruits but only cooked, and if one eats them fresh, one should take care to peel them. At last one should eat lightly, but beware of fasting. When there is a plague about, one should never go outside the house between the hours of six and seven in the evening, and if one does, walk only on the sides of the street and not its middle.

A remedy for plague – hang white onion and garlic in every window of the house and every doorway, and on every wall. Or else, eat nine grains of mustard every day on an empty stomach, or dry every day a piece of bread and bear it in a pocket.

Pox

The citron fruit is helpful for small children sick with pox.

Pregnancy

If a woman sees a horse early in her pregnancy, she would not give birth for twelve months, but if she passes three times under a pregnant mare, her ill fortune would go to the horse and she would not miscarry. A pregnant woman should take care not to eat any spoiled foods while expecting so to not harm her child. She should also avoid eating saffron while pregnant.

A woman who miscarried before should, before trying to conceive, first take the shell of an egg from which a chick hatched, grind it to powder and drink the powder with water. If a woman does not feel her child move within her womb, she should eat many sweet almonds.

These are remedies for ensuring that a woman never miscarry. She should drink the ashes of a burned snake, or carry a snake's shed skin on her while pregnant, or the heel of a rat, or the heart of a rabbit dried by smoke, or carry with her a scorpion inside a tube sealed with wax.

Should a woman have a difficult labor, she should drink every quarter of an hour a spoonful of milk from a breastfeeding woman, and best if mixed with egg yolk. Or else, mix a spoonful of the ashes of a burned frog with wine or with water and let her drink. Another remedy – to take dried horse dung with wine or water and let her drink without her knowledge. And another - to take dry droppings of pigeon, burn half a spoonful by her, and the rest cook in wine and let the woman drink.

If the child is dead and the woman is having difficulties birthing it, she should drink a woman's milk with honey heated to clarity, a spoonful every quarter of an hour.

If a woman eats boiled eggs while pregnant, her children's eyes would be fair. If she eats lettuce, they would be beautiful and healthy-looking. If she eats citrons, they would have a pleasant smell – there is a tale of a girl whose mother ate so many citrons bearing her that her smell was heavenly and they would call her to her father whenever he wished to refresh his breath, rather than bother with perfumes. While pregnant, a woman should avoid eating saffron, or her children would have unhealthy skin.

These are the ways to ensure the birth of a son – one, the woman should drink wolf's gall, or put a drop of gall in her nose. Two, she should take a little of the navel of another woman's son and mix it with honey and sweet-scented water, drink some of it and the rest put in a small bottle of silver she would carry with her. Three, that the couple's bed be placed with its front and back facing east and west, and its sides facing north and south. Four, that the woman should take gall of cow and soak it in some wool that she would carry in her mouth before her period. Five, that she should take the afterbirth of a cow and dry it well in the sun, then grind it to powder, and mix it with wine to drink while she gives birth. Hereafter she would bear only sons.

And this is a last sure thing – a woman may take the brain of a male sparrow and put it in her vagina before lying with her husband, and after giving birth, take some of the cord and give it dried to the chickens to eat. If a rooster eats them, she would henceforth bear sons, and if the hen – she would bear daughters.

To help a woman become pregnant, she should take a rabbit's skin and burn it, then drink the ashes in a cup of wine every morning for nine days. Or else, the woman should make a small bowl of wax and fill it with the blood of her menstruation, cover it and bury it under the roots of an apple tree bearing fresh fruit. Then she would become pregnant, and the tree would bear no more fruit. Another remedy – that the woman should not carry on her body quicksilver, which acts against fertility. And a fourth – that if man and wife are healthy, the woman should take a male pigeon and a female one and take out their brains straight after slaughter. Then she should sit in her bed and put the brains in her womb for an hour, and after that hour lie with her husband and she will become pregnant.

Prison

If a man is to be imprisoned, he should drink a cup of wine toasting life with three of those who live him, and they should bless him that he should soon go free.

Proverbs

These are some that everyone should know:

As a donkey would climb a ladder, so would wisdom be found in fools.

As a lamb should dwell with the tiger, so should a woman dwell with her mother-in-law.

If you should find a crow all white, so you would find wisdom in a woman.

Rags

Wearing a rag in times of trouble is a helpful costume. One who dresses in rags would be saved from his doom and his wish for better times be granted.

Rheumatism

This is a chronic disease that causes joint pains and aches in the muscles and soft tissue surrounding them. One remedy for the pain it causes is to put honey on the aching joint and on the honey, thinly ground white mustard. Then bind the joint with linen. Another is to grind some lime into small pieces, put it in a bottle of glass, pour wine on it and put it in the sun for three days, mixing the liquid in the bottle some times every day. Then, after the three days, filter the wine well and put it in a new bottle and close it well. This liquid should be applied to the aching joint twice a day. Eating grape pits should ease the pain of stiff joints, as does smearing rat's blood on one's body.

Salt

There are many different types of salt.

Salt made of earth and water.

Salt from the mountains or the depths of the earth. This might be white or black.

Salt that is dug from the ground in great precious stones.

Salt that is mined in the mountains and has several scented types, black or bright white, or red, or green.

Heavenly salt is the salt that came on Sodom from the sky. Earthly salt comes from the ground, and sometimes from metals like gold and copper.

There is a salt that is found in drinks like wine, oil, vinegar and honey.

Salt that is found in plants, trees, fruits and roots of grass.

Salt from animals.

Sea

For one who travels by sea and fears the weather – he should eat a whole onion before boarding the ship.

Seed

Spilling seed in vain is a terrible sin, and it is said of one who spills his seed on the ground:

That he will be slain.

That he has all but spilt blood

That he shall not come into the presence of the Lord.

That he causes him and his sons to be exiled.

That he should come to poverty.

That he brings famine to his people.

That he does not rise when the dead are resurrected.

That he causes there to be in the world death and plague.

And this aside from the punishment he would suffer in hell.

Skin

For all blemishes on the skin of the ear or finger caused by cold, warm linen oil and wax on an open fire, then mix with egg yolk, all in equal amounts. Put the paste on a cloth and put on the blemish twice a day.

For facial skin problems, a good remedy is to take pigeon droppings dried white and cook with sheep milk until you have a thick paste, then put this on a cloth which you must put on your face at night. Do this for several nights and the face would be clean and the skin shining.

Sleep

One who cannot sleep for no reason should put a linen pouch filled with moist salt on his head, and if the salt dries wet it again.

For a tendency to speak during sleep, a person should wear a dog's tooth around his neck. If one shouts in his sleep because of bad dreams that cause him to wake, that is because the body has some need that is remedied by waking. Perhaps he sleeps with his hand on his heart and causes his breath to be short, or perhaps this is because of weakness of nerves or some depression. Such dreams are not ill in themselves. If you put the tooth of a dead man or the bone of his left arm by a sleeping man's head, he would not wake until you take the tooth or bone away.

Snakes

If a man is bitten by a snake, he should hurry and drink from a river, before the snake can reach it, and so the snake would die and the man live. One who carries the head of a snake in his belt – no harm may come to him. Another remedy is to swallow seven fleas born in summer, or to place a chicken's brain on the bite. For a woman, she should take the seed of her husband in a cloth, soak it in warm water and put it on the bite.

Snoring

Aside from its noise, snoring can cause discomfort in sleep until the sleeper wakes, or cause the one who snores to choke in his sleep. A remedy for this is to mix a spoonful of sugar with egg yolk put it in a glass of hot milk and drink it three times a day for several days.

Speech

One whose power of speech disappeared suddenly should put citron peel in his mouth. For a child whose speech is gone from some sickness or fright, his mother should put a finger of her right hand within her womb until it is warm, then quickly put it into the child's mouth.

Spleen

A remedy for pain in the spleen –take the brain of a rabbit, male for a man and female for a woman, squeeze and grind it till it is made into a paste, then smear on a cloth and bandage the aching place for six hours. This lowers swelling in the spleen. And another remedy – take five droppings of sheep mixed with strong vinegar and put on a cloth, and bandage the aching place from time to time over a few days, till the pain passes.

This to cure children and youth –take a spleen of a cow, male for a boy and female for a girl, and cut it along its length, till a sort of ring is made. Then pass the child's body through the ring, from head to toe, three times. Then hang the spleen in a warm place and engulf it in smoke, and when the cow spleen dries, the child's spleen would be healed.

Stomach

This for a swollen stomach – cook a living frog with oil in a new pot of clay, until the oil is halfway gone and the frog is soft like thick paste. Spread that paste on the stomach, and if the swelling goes down to the legs, spread it on these as well. Pears are good against diseases of the stomach, as are nut oil and chestnuts and cumin. Stomachaches can be cured by drinking willow bark cooked with red or white wine and pepper, or rosemary cooked in wine. Compresses of woman's milk and juniper juice are also helpful.

Strawberries

These fruits soften the stomach. From them is made a sort of jam good for cleansing the throat and soothing any pain there. The strawberry's roots, when ground, remove belly worms, and the leaves, when ground, are a cure for all skin diseases.

Success

This to become successful – every person, from time to time, finds coins on the ground. They should pick up these coins and not spend them, but keep them in a pocket set aside for that purpose.

For success in a trial, a man should hold a small gem under his tongue while the trial proceeds. Or else, he should hold in his right hand a small mezuzah.

To be successful in business, be sure, whenever you speak of your business, to say before it "God willing", in whatever business you turn to.

Sweat

A remedy for causing a sick man to sweat, thus lowering his fever – take some oats and cook them well with vinegar, and when they are softened, wrap them in bandages on the sick man's stomach and he would sweat. There are healthy men who for some reason or another sweat overly much at night, and lose their strength and become thin. These would be healed by often washing themselves with fish oil.

Teeth

For an aching tooth that is whole and healthy, take salt and pepper ground thin in a metal spoon or a bowl and mix it with wine. Then light the wine until the fire dies out and all that is left is a red juice. Soak the juice in a cloth and put it on the tooth. This remedy is good also for a hole in the tooth. Or else, mix flour, honey and much salt and pepper, and put the paste on the aching tooth. The resulting saliva will ease the pain.

Throat

For an aching throat because of some disease, one should soak a cloth in cold salty water, then wrap it around the neck, and on this wear a thick woolen cloth. The cloth must be soaked again every three hours until the pain is eased. Or else, soak the cloth with wine mixed with cold water, and wash the throat with cold water several times.

Trees

Plenty of trees are in this world, some bear fruit, some are scented, and some, both that and that. They are all needed in this world, all have a place. They all provide for God's creatures, animals and men. From the trees, fruits and herbs do men produce food and medicine, and they have great hidden qualities, also, remedies for many things.

Apple: To cure all ailments of the stomach, cook the fruit in vinegar that is then soaked into a cloth, and place the cloth on the stomach. Waters drawn from the tree while young and green make a woman's face fair and attractive to her husband. Boiling the wood makes a remedy that clears the eyes. Cloth soaked with it put on the navel would stop bloody diarrhea or a woman's period, and also cure infections of the eyelids, mouth, ears and many others.

Castor: A medicinal tree. From its dried flowers is made a powder good for stopping diarrhea, from its leaves, when cooked, is made a remedy for bringing a woman's delayed period, though this use is not recommended since it might strike her barren. Water in which castor wood was boiled is good for diseases of the liver, kidneys and spleen, and also for the skin. Its leaves have a quality that cools burns and draws dirty blood and pus from them.

Chestnut: The nuts strengthen the stomach and ease digestion, but might cause bad breath. They can work as aphrodisiacs. The peel, the bark of the tree and its roots heal any blow or bruise.

Citron: A fruit of many merits, both fair to behold and to eat. Its peel soothes any internal pain and gives strength. Its juicy inner part cools the liver and helps digestion. It quenches thirst and works against sweat, and might do well for children suffering from chicken pox.

Frankincense: Mentioned often in the Bible. The powder of its bark or branches, mixed with water and drunk, is a remedy for infections in the ligaments and in the kidneys and bladder. Should a woman drink it mixed with the urine of a female mule, she would not become pregnant. The fruits soothe earaches. The flowers, ground when young and mixed with honey, sharpen one's eyesight, and from them is made a paste that ease pains and puts to sleep.

Henna: Strengthens the skin, and has many merits.

Lemon: Good for all diseases of the stomach, and against every illness besides.

Myrtle: The fruits cause constipation and are thus useful against diarrhea, and give strength. Myrtle cures excess sweating and can be used to treat hernia.

Nut: The juice squeezed from a nut's wet shell may be good for induced vomiting, and is also good for washing the mouth and throat. The oil of nuts is good for any illness and affliction. A person whose stomach aches would be healed by drinking it.

Olive: Olive oil is healthy and good applied to any wound or disease of the skin. Its pit, if ground down and mixed with honey, cures bruises, burns and wounds inside the mouth.

Peach: Remedies can be made from its roots, trunk or leaves. Its fruit and flowers as well are all good for killing belly worms. If cooked together, they make eye drops that heal infections and dimness in the eyes. From its bark and leaves a paste can be made that stops hair from falling out. The tree's resin, if mixed with red wine, may heal diseases of the lungs, the throat and kidneys, cures kidney stones and clears urine. It is a good remedy even for a person who is coughing blood.

Pear: This tree grows around the eggs that animals lay in its bark, creating a place for them to hatch. Because of that, the fruits of this tree and foods made from them are good for diseases of the stomach and of the womb. The wood can be ground to powder, mixed with egg yolk and applied to an aching limb for immediate relief. If the powder is cooked, drinking the mixture stops bleeding from any part of the body.

Pomegranate: Of this fruit there are two types, sweet and sour. The sour pomegranates stop diarrhea, slack thirst, cool the liver and strengthen the stomach, while the sweet ones soften it, but both make a person's heart merry. The bark of both trees causes constipation if cooked in water or wine, or if ground to powder. There is another type of tree that gives no fruits, but only rose-like flowers, and its ashes are recommended to clear all infections of the skin.

Poplar: If its bark is cut, water oozes from this tree.

Drinking it, especially in the month of May, is a cure for kidney stones and soothes the bladder. This water is good also for washing the mouth and throat and removing blemishes on the skin, and for diseases of the blood. There is a story of an old man who was leprous, who drank these waters for forty days and was healed completely.

Prune: Cooked, its fruits soften the stomach and quench thirst, and its wood or bark are good for washing the mouth and throat. Doctors praise its leaves and fruits as useful for treating urinary diseases.

Rose: Many types of roses make many remedies, however, they all give strength to the body and make the heart joyful. The red rose stops diarrhea, while the white may cause it.

Rosemary: A medicinal wood according to doctors as well. Cooking the wood itself and its leaves makes remedies for many things. The flowers are good against weakness of the ligaments, paralysis and epileptic seizures as well as burns. Its ash soothes toothaches and cleans the teeth. The bark and leaves are good for washing the hair to give it strength and shine, against any skin problems, and to banish foul smells.

Vine: Grapes cool the body, slack thirst and stop diarrhea when they are only barely ripe. When too ripe however, they cause diarrhea and weaken the body. Raisins strengthen the innards, but may cause one to gain weight.

The seeds ease joint aches. If wine is cooked until it is thick like honey, it soothes the stomach and helps fight off any affliction. The ash of burned vine roots can singe the flesh and cause burns.

Willow: There are three types of willow, each with its own name. The leaves of this tree cool the body and dry it, and doctors recommend cooking it with wine and adding some pepper to cure diseases of the intestines. In them is a juice that one can wash the feet with to bring sleep, to lower fever or stop nosebleeds. If the leaves are scattered around a sick man's bed, they cool the air there and may break the fever.

Urine

To help a man who is having difficulties urinating, grind barley seeds well and pour the powder in strong vinegar without cooking, then let him drink of it and he would be cured. Or else bathe the man in water in which oats were cooked. And another remedy – let the man drink bitter almonds and goat milk together several times. Cinnamon, watermelons and dates cooked with dried figs are all good for helping a man urinate.

A woman who cannot urinate should put within her womb the powder of ground sweet almonds.

One who cannot hold his urine, and especially at night in his bed, should for a full month take baths in water mixed with small chunks of sulfur. Or else, he should take the dried bladder of a ram and burn it, then drink the ashes with red wine. And a third, that he should burn the hooves of goats and drink the ashes mixed with wine for three days.

Other cures – cook a rabbit's brain in wine and mix with vinegar and water and drink the mix on an empty stomach for two days, or to cover the man's penis with a mix of eggshell and sugar, which he should also eat in the mornings after a hot bath.

Also one can burn chicken's dung and put the ashes in the man's food or drink without his knowledge to help him hold his urine.

A man who urinates in his bed at night should keep his head lower than his feet by putting bricks under his feet in the bed. Or else he should drink ram's blood mixed with woman's milk for three nights before going to bed. And another remedy for that – to cut out the wet patch of cloth, burn it, mix the ashes with wine and drink.

One who suffers from any disease of the bladder should not drink any alcoholic drinks. To be cured, they may crush a wasp in a glass of water and drink, or put in water ground watermelon and onion seeds and drink.

Venom

A sure remedy for the venom of a bee or wasp – once the sting is removed, put a slice of onion on the spot, or crush the sting and put it on the stung place.

For all sorts of venom, sure remedies are dried nuts, hot olive oil, saffron, or fresh eggs eaten first thing in the morning. The mixture of a live crab ground down mixed with she-ass's milk is helpful against the venom of scorpions, snakes and spiders.

Weather

These are the signs in the animal kingdom that it is about to rain:

If the fish swim close to the surface or jump on it.

If flies pester the flocks in their cowsheds and barns.

If the pigs roll in the mud or dig through their food with their snouts.

If the cats lick their paws and wipe their eyes, which shine.

If the dogs walk faster, stomping their feet.

If the geese float on the water, spreading their wings wide, and at times dip their heads in the water.

If bats fly close to the ground or to water.

And these are the signs by moon, sun, clouds and fog:

If in the morning the sun is red or many-colored.

If the sun becomes white in the east or the west.

If after sunset the sky is cloudless and the stars very bright.

If there is a red cloud in the sky during sunset, it would rain the next day.

If the sun is clouded during sunrise, and if the clouds are red, it would rain in the evening.

If during sunset the sun takes on a bluish tinge, or is surrounded by dark clouds.

If the mountains are covered by fog, or by clouds coming from the north.

If the sun is surrounded by thick clouds, dark from the south and bright from the north.

If the moon is dark and surrounded by a ring of clouds.

If a fog rises from the ground in the morning.

And if during the rain the sky is colored blue and red, that is a sign that there would be more rain soon.

And these are the signs that a clear day is to follow:

If the clouds are red at sunset.

If at sunset and sunrise small clouds are about the sun.

If the clouds scatter during sunrise.

If the sky is clear before dawn.

If the moon shines very brightly.

If the morning mists turn to fog.

If the sun turns red from the west after the rain.

Will

A man should not write his will at the last moment, when ill or dying, but when still clear of mind and aware of what he wishes to write in it, before anything happens, God forbid, to make him die suddenly.

One should order one's children in the will to follow one's ways and do the things that one would have done in life.

Wisdom

Wisdom and clarity of the mind depend on eating. Those who eat fine food and drink fine drinks are wise men, and those who eat crude food as villagers who eat oats, onions and the likes have minds that are dull.

This for one who wishes to grow wise – not to read a book that he takes up once, but many times. To read once, or twice, is not enough, for whenever a book is read again, a new thing of it is revealed to the reader. The more books one reads, the wiser would one grow. A man's wisdom is only as great as the number of books he has read. Thus it is a good thing to purchase many books and read as many types and sorts of books as a man is able.

Witchcraft

Some ask if there is witchcraft in the world. To this, Kabbala says that denying it is impossible, for witchcraft of sorts is mentioned in the Bible, and there is even an order to kill all witches and soothsayers and other such dabblers in magic. Denying the existence of witchcraft is thus denying the Bible.

There are many different types of witchcraft – there are those whose magic comes from the stars, and others who draw it from snakes which they eat and tell the future.

Others put bones of animals in their mouths and then can foresee events, and yet others do the same through a mirror. But all come to an ill end, and all suffer constant weariness.

To ward against witchcraft, take seven sparrow chicks from seven nests, burn them, and with their ashes you can banish every spell.

A remedy to cancel the effects of a spell – eat a fish that was found within another fish if it is not yet rotten. Or else take the afterbirth of a newborn baby and wash it well in water, then wash in that same water the body of the victim of the spell.

Another remedy – that the victim of the spell be enveloped in the smoke from the burning heart of a fish, or the burning cockscomb of a rooster. The cockscomb must be taken straightway after the rooster is killed and burned on hot coals, or else burned with the brain of a rooster or a hen for a woman. The victim must inhale the smoke into his nose.

And another – to take a bowl in which the victim urinated and put burning embers in it and on them some dry grass and also some feathers from the blanket the victim uses at night. Then the victim of the spell must urinate on the embers and throw them away.

Worms

There is a type of worms that eats books, and a type of parasites that live in the human body. Of this second type there are worms that live in the intestines and worms that live by the anus, especially in children. There are many remedies to be rid of these.

For worms that consume books, a good remedy is to put some drops of turpentine inside the books and around the shelves, or in a bowl on the shelf. The scent of it soaks into the wood of the shelf and into the books, and kills the worms.

This is a remedy for worms in a child's stomach, to put peeled onions in water for a whole night, then let the child drink the waters. Or else to cook ground garlic with milk and let the child drink. And another – to take some flour and mix it with cow gall until a sort of dough is formed, then fry that dough in butter. Put the fried dough on the child's stomach while still warm and leave it there for time to time.

Adults too suffer from worms. There is a kind that sucks moisture that the body needs, and may grow very long, until when it lacks for place, it releases pieces of itself to be extracted from the body. It latches inside the stomach and is very hard to be rid of, since so long as its head remains it may grow again. There is a cure for this worm that can only be given by a doctor.

Worry

Not only Kabbala but also medical lore tells us that worry is the worst of diseases, that it brings a man close to old age.

Before his death, it is told, Alexander the Great wrote in a letter to his mother: "Do not be sorrowful at the day of my death. As soon as you learn of my death, order a great feast to be made, and call to it all the kings and lords, and make it a day of merriment. But order it told to those summoned that into that feast cannot enter a man who has seen sorrow or ill fortune plague him, so there would be no grief mingled with that merriment. I wish it to be a day of complete joy with no sadness." The day she learned of his death, Alexander's mother did all that he ordered, summoned and prepared all that was needed for the feast, and ordered all lords and kings to come to it. When it was time, not one man came to the feast. When she asked why none came, she was told – you have ordered that no man should come to the feast who met grief and ill fortune, and these met any man in his time, and so none came. Then Alexander's mother spoke and said: "Alexander, my son, you are wise from your beginning to your end, for you wished to comfort me by showing me that grief is no new thing, and that all men meet with sorrow."

There is not a man alive who does not feel sorry, envy and so on.

Wounds

To heal a wound, take some flour with honey in a thick paste, and put it on the wound. Or else for a wound that is hot and filled with pus, take a spoonful of butter and warm it on a fire until it becomes a clear liquid. This mix with egg yolk and let it cool until you have a paste, that you should put on a bandage for the wound. This it is said to be a remedy for a wound from which pus runs for many days – to take the feces of a baby that is still suckling, put it on a rag and bandage the wound with it.

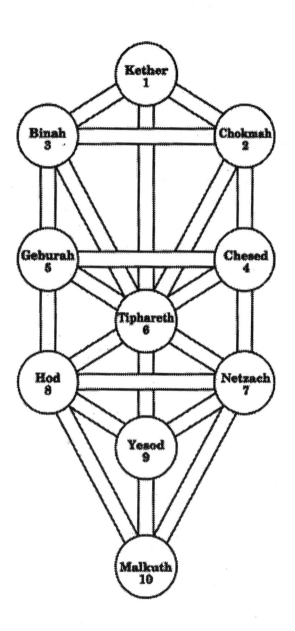